A Remembrance of Eden

A Remembrance of Eden

Harriet Bailey Bullock Daniel's Memories
of a Frontier Plantation in Arkansas, 1849–1872

Edited with an Introduction by

Margaret Jones Bolsterli

The University of Arkansas Press
Fayetteville   1993

03   02   01   00   99   5   4   3   2   1

Designer: Ellen Beeler
Typeface: Perpetua

The paper used in this publication meets the minimum requirements of the
American National Standard for Permanence of Paper for Printed Library Materials
Z39.48-1984. ♾

Library of Congress Cataloging-in-Publication Data

Daniel, Harriet Bailey Bullock.
   A remembrance of Eden: Harriet Bailey Bullock Daniel's memories of a frontier
   plantation in Arkansas, 1849–1872 / edited with an introduction by Margaret Jones
   Bolsterli.

      p.   cm.
   Includes bibliographical references.
   ISBN 1-55728-290-0 (cloth : alk. paper)
   ISBN 1-55728-589-6 (pbk : alk. paper)
     1. Plantation life—Arkansas—History—19th century.   2. Slavery—
Arkansas.   3. Arkansas—History—Civil War, 1861–1865—Personal narratives.
4. United States—History—Civil War, 1861–1865—Personal narratives,
Confederate.   5. Arkansas—Social life and customs.   6. Daniel, Harriet Bailey
Bullock.   I. Bolsterli, Margeret Jones.   II. Title.
F411.D165 1993
976.7'04—dc20   93-6787
                                                CIP

For
the memory of
Alice Goodridge Daniel

For Bailey Webb

And for Willard B. Gatewood, Jr.
"il miglior fabbro"

Acknowledgments

Because everything fell into place so easily, preparing this book has been one of the most pleasant tasks of my academic career, and I am grateful for the assistance of those who made it so. The first acknowledgement should go to the late Alice Goodridge Daniel, Harriet Bailey Bullock Daniel's daughter, who encouraged her mother to write down the stories she had been telling for almost sixty years. Alice was the first editor, arranging, transcribing, and making copies of the episodic memoirs for the members of the family. Dr. Bailey Webb, Bailey Daniel's granddaughter, started the manuscript on its path toward publication that led, through the hands of Professor Robert Durden of Duke University and Professor Willard B. Gatewood, Jr., of the University of Arkansas, finally to me. Dr. Webb also generously provided family photographs and arranged for photocopies of the Daniel family letters to be sent to me by Perkins Library, Duke University. This assistance from Duke University Library is gratefully acknowledged. Professor Ann Field Alexander, of Mary Baldwin College, Bailey Daniel's great-granddaughter, offered personal encouragement and professional advice.

Members of the Arkansas branch of the Bullock family who still live in Manchester community, Clara, Claude, and Neill McCaskill lent family photographs and showed me around the site of Sylvan Home. Neill McCaskill also made valuable drawings of the site and floor plans of the house as it was built. Clara

McCaskill made two trips to the court house in Hempstead County to verify family holdings there.

Florence Blakely, retired Reference Librarian at Duke University Library, made early identifications of people and places mentioned in the manuscript. Jo Wright, at First Presbyterian Church in Arkadelphia, was helpful in arranging the loan of Charles L. Bullock's portrait for reproduction. Wendy Richter, at Ouachita Baptist University Library found valuable material for me. Col. H.B. Arnold, of the Clark County Historical Association, gave useful information in a telephone conversation. Members of the staff of Special Collections, Mullins Library, University of Arkansas, were most helpful in finding elusive information and hauling out heavy manuscript census records.

Willard B. Gatewood, Jr., and Olivia Sordo offered encouragement and editorial suggestions as they have for my work over the course of many years.

Finally, I want to acknowledge my debt of gratitude to Fulbright College of Arts and Sciences, University of Arkansas, for the semester's leave of absence from teaching that allowed me to complete this work so quickly. It was a generous gift of time and money.

—Margaret Jones Bolsterli
1992

Contents

List of Illustrations and Figures

(following page 80)

Introduction

The Nature of the Document

In 1929, Alice Goodridge Daniel asked her eighty-year-old mother to write down the memories of her childhood that she had been telling her children and grandchildren for almost sixty years. She thought, in daughterly fashion, that she had hit upon the perfect combination of busywork for a lonely old woman and the preservation of treasured family stories. At its most basic level, this is what she got.

But the importance of the document that Harriet Bailey Bullock Daniel set down and that Alice saved is so much more than merely a matter of familial interest that its significance fairly leaps off the page into the ordering historical and literary mind. For what we have here is no less than a window onto the collective memory of a people. So much so, that the reader has an eerie feeling of having been here before, of having been in this place and having met these people, as indeed we all have, for reading this memoir is like reading the ur-text of southern literature. The stories that "Bailey," as her family called her, had spent a lifetime telling were from the same pool of experience that produced the stories told to most southern children up to the present generation. Among others, little Margaret Mitchell in Georgia and little William Faulkner in Mississippi were hearing versions of them at about the same time that Mrs. Daniel was telling them to her children. Mothers told stories like these while busy with other things. The mind wanders while the hands are mixing batter, or sewing, or churning, or ironing and what more likely place for it to return to than a lost Eden. It is difficult to imagine Eve talking about much else.

With the clear eyes of a child, Bailey observed one of the most exciting eras in American history: within a score of years she witnessed the civilizing of the frontier, the blossoming of a plantation in the midst of primeval forest, the spectacle of war brought as close as a division of Confederate soldiers, complete with two brigadier generals and a full colonel, camped in the front grove could bring it, then the dramatic loss of the war and its aftermath when the little girl who had never fastened her own shoes or brushed her own hair faced a brave new world in which everyone had to work. Little wonder that Bailey ends her account in 1872 with her marriage and removal to North Carolina. Paradise was over. "Sylvan Home," the plantation in Arkansas, had become for her the lost garden all southerners like to imagine in their backgrounds, a matter of interest to us all, not just Bailey Bullock Daniel's descendants.

In addition to its appeal to the literary imagination, Bailey Daniel's account of life on this frontier plantation fits a number of categories interesting to social historians. She provides material enlightening to anyone interested in The Great Migration, the institution of slavery, women's history, the southern home front during the Civil War, the domestic economy of a well-run plantation, the religious and medical practices of a planter family, southern agricultural history and Arkansas History.

Although Bailey, who was born after the family arrived in Arkansas, did not make The Great Migration, she shows us two significant things about it: first of all, she describes in detail the pot of gold at the end of the rainbow, the financial reasons why a man like her father, Charles Lewis Bullock, who was successful where he was, would risk such a venture. And she illuminates what might be called the phenomenon of "progressive settlement" that resulted from making the westward migration in different legs so that ultimately, when a family reached its permanent place its ties were not to the original place of settlement on the Eastern Seaboard, but to the midpoint of the journey in Tennessee, Alabama, Mississippi, etc. For the ten or twelve years that the Bullocks spent in Tennessee they probably looked back to North Carolina, while becoming enmeshed in a support system in Tennessee. When they arrived in Arkansas, their deepest ties were with Tennessee, not North Carolina, despite their having numerous family members still in North Carolina. By the time the Bullocks got to Arkansas, the Eastern Seaboard had become a distant country; there were too many memories not associated with it. The standard of comparison for the new frontier in Arkansas was the old frontier in Tennessee. The Bullock children were sent back to school in Somerville, Tennessee, and two of the older daughters married and remained there. If Bailey had not married a first cousin and gone back to North Carolina, it is conceivable that the remaining frail threads of communication between the Bullocks and people in that state would have been completely broken.

If the Bullocks did indeed land in the Garden of Eden when they reached Arkansas, slavery was the built-in serpent that would bring about its destruction and cast a curse on its perpetrators for generations to come. Bailey Daniel's stories of her childhood cover some ground in the history of slavery not covered before in an account of an Arkansas plantation. At this distance in time it is difficult to comprehend that slavery existed, that human beings, particularly Americans, could have legally *owned* other human beings. The mind recoils from this knowledge and welcomes a voice from that shadowy region of our past that sheds some light on the logistics of the arrangements between masters and slaves. "How did it work?" we wonder, and while Bailey doesn't answer directly, she gives us enough information to allow us to draw some conclusions that, perhaps, complicate the picture even more.

The nature of the relationship between the Bullocks and their slaves had many aspects of an extended family. No matter what they thought of one another and no matter what the legal arrangements were, these people, regardless of color, were bound together not only by present necessity, but also by a common past. Some of the slaves at Sylvan Home had begun the westward migration with the Bullocks in North Carolina in 1835 or so. An undated letter, which can be placed by internal evidence at about 1888, from Sister Nannie at Sylvan Home to Bailey in North Carolina, carries the following poignant information about some of their former slaves:

> Aunts Clary, Rachel, Patsy and Rose are still living. Aunt Patsy would be glad to hear from any of her kin. I have forgotten the names of those she knew fifty years ago. Suppose (you) will find no trace of them and mention it to please her.[1]

These people, white and black, formed permanent parts of each others' lives. When Bailey Daniel was past seventy-five years of age, she was able to compose a poem listing the names of fifty-two slaves. The following two letters to her from her old nurse Eliza indicate the mutuality of this affection that has endured over a period of some sixty-five years. The letters are in pencil, on lined paper, in a clear hand that is presumably Eliza's own since she does not state otherwise. The "Mister Charlie," "Charlie," or "Charles" mentioned is Bailey's youngest brother, Charles Lewis Bullock, Jr. Other letters mention that one of Bailey's nicknames was "Buck."

Witherspoon, Ark
Mar 19th '17

My Dear Miss Harriett

    I have thought of you often, so often & wish that I could see you again. Charles was here a few days since & he gave me your address. I am well am living with a family named Howard. They came here from Chicago 22 yrs since & I have been living with them for past 18 yrs. I am a widow but have a good home with the Howards. Miss Harriett I wish you would please tell me my age. Only 3 of us are left now. Martha Ann, & Tilda & me. The balance are all gone. I wrote to Miss Katie but didn't get any reply & wondered why until Charlie told me she was dead. I have but one child, a daughter, lives about a mile from me. I will be so glad to hear from you. I feel young & am very little gray & everybody says I look young & I sure am taking the very best of care of myself now. I wish you would please write to me for I will be overjoyed to hear from you. I used snuff for a good many years but it was injurious to me & I quit it absolutely six years ago and haven't touched it since. With much love and best wishes always I am your

Old Slave Gal
Eliza Bullock

Witherspoon, Ark
Apr 4, '17

My Dear Miss Buck

    Yrs 25th since rec'd & I sure was glad to hear from you & to know you are well & so pleasantly situated and where you say I just cried I had to stop and have a cry too & in reading a letter from you makes me feel just like I was in our old home.

Silla was older than Line & I came next to Line now about how old would that make me? Henry is dead but Jerry is alive yet. All of Aunt Rachaels gals but Martha Ann are dead. I sign my name Bullock for I couldn't feel right or get along satisfactorily with any other name & I feel more at home with that name. Jim Jones died 17 yrs since & Aunt Rachael & Aunt Rose are dead. Mister Charlie owns & is operating a saw mill at Dalark, Ark, Aunt Polly Smith & Betsy Ann Goodlow & Harriet Bullock & Vick are all dead. Yes, I have to laugh about your going bare headed. We just couldn't keep a bonnet on your head & sometimes would have to hunt all over the place for your bonnet liable to find it under the house or anywhere in or out of the yard. Uncle Oscar is dead but his Sam is alive yet. Harry is alive yet as is Nancy & she lives about 2 miles south of here. My health continues good but I sure do take the best of care of myself and I get everything I ever need with the Howards. Charlie is well liked by Mr & Mrs Howard. He always comes to see us all when in our neighborhood. Take the best of care of yourself & I won't forget you in my prayers & I will always be overjoyed to hear from you. I wonder if you remember the day we buried our little Ladd dog in the front yard. Well Goodbye & you have my love & best wishes always. I am a Baptist & try to do good every day.

Your old Girl
Liza Bullock[2]

There is no discernible difference in tone between these two letters and those in the collection of family letters written to Bailey by her sisters, nieces and nephews.

The relationship between the Bullocks and their slaves was complex and astonishingly close. After reading accounts such as this, it becomes more and more difficult to rationalize the past reluctance of scholars to credit the reciprocal transference of culture between the races. Parents tried to minimize the opportunities for influence of the slaves on the white children but, according to this evidence, to little avail. Both Bailey and her black friends, children and grown-ups alike, are always on the lookout for Mr. Bullock, who will put a stop to Bailey's participation in the slave activities; but his vigilance does not work; she never stops playing the slave children's games and eating their food. It is worth noting that she only once mentions playing with white children, except siblings, and that on the occasion of being taken to the spa at Tulip by Sister Nannie who knew she would spend all her time with the "little negroes" if left at home without her older sister's supervision.

Her world had more blacks than whites in it, and they did not even disappear at night to leave a clear path for white culture to sweep away the influence of the day. When a visiting cousin gets religion in the middle of the night, Mr. Bullock sends the slaves kept sleeping on the dining room floor for just such emergencies for a choir of black men to come sing for "Miss Martha." They come up from the quarters and stand around the Bullocks in bed in the master bedroom singing and praying until Miss Martha is eased, then they troop back home. How much deeper could ties of community *be*? And yet, Mr. Bullock has a foreman who beats them until the blood soaks their clothes and he himself, stern Presbyterian that he is, can lose his temper and lash the beloved cook with a horsewhip because his ersatz coffee is not clear.

When Eugene Genovese's *Roll, Jordan, Roll* came out in 1974 and told about little slave children being fed at troughs in the plantation yards, scholars were horrified. Yet here is a little girl from the Big House eating peas and pork out of the communal skillet in the yard with a mussel shell *and loving it*. Bailey remembered the fine taste of those peas for the rest of her life. She is dosed by the slave nurse just as the black children are. When she can't remember the way a hymn should go, she asks Aunt Rose, who was at the service too, to teach her so she can teach it to the little black children with whom she is "playing church." She is there at the hog killing, broiling hog liver over the fire with the black children; she spends her days in the slave nursery. On and on goes the catalogue of the daily contacts Bailey had with black people. How could she not have been influenced by their speech and tastes in food, by the very thought patterns of these people who were her constant companions?

Perhaps it was this closeness to the slaves as little girls that led to deeper sympathies between white women and black people. Joan Cashin in *A Family Venture: Men and Women on the Southern Frontier* notes that while there were some cruel and abusive slave mistresses, "Abusing slaves was never part and parcel of the female sex role as it was of the male sex role because women were not encouraged to demonstrate their prowess by dominating other people."[3]

Bailey lets us see, with her, that slaves had certain rights; when she steals Aunt Rachel's apples, she is confident of being whipped by her father unless she is clever enough to buy Aunt Rachel off with something more valuable than the apples or the satisfaction of seeing the thief punished. There is always a certain amount of tension in this memoir between the pulls of conflicting loyalties. Bailey loves the slaves and she loves her father, so we are forced to imagine what it is like for her when she has to throw her little body between him and Aunt 'Riah to stop a whipping. His response is interesting; he wonders what he is to do with such a child! She should not step in to mitigate the exercise of his paternal authority, which is absolute for both slaves and children.

Another area of antebellum life illuminated by Bailey's memories lies in the women's sphere. Until recently, we have not known much about what the women were doing while the men were taming the forests, making or losing fortunes, fighting wars and doing all those things proscribed to women because of gender. Although recent works like Catherine Clinton's *The Plantation Mistress* and Elizabeth Fox-Genovese's *Within the Plantation Household* have done much to fill the gaps in our knowledge about this period of women's history, individual accounts still add new bits of information. And Bailey Daniel's memoir is, above all else, a woman's account. Although she had a lively mind and was interested in everything her circumscribed world had to offer, her activities were so limited by expectations for females that many things were simply outside her powers of observation. But she tells us in some detail what the women and girls were doing and reaffirms what Scarlett O'Hara told us: Learning to be a southern belle has its problems too. One gets hungry on the limited amount of food allowed for a perfect figure and tightening stays until the ribs lap over can be a factor in an early death, as seems to have been the case with Sister Mary Helen. Bailey enjoyed the surreptitious food she had with the slaves so much because she was literally hungry. It was unseemly for an upper class white girl to show hunger by eating much at meals and it was unthinkable that one might be fat.

Charles Bullock wanted his daughters to have accomplishments that would make them interesting wives and mothers but even a job as genteel as teaching school, if it were done for money, was considered by his family to be demeaning. It is ironic that when Bailey's stepmother, in tears, asked a Union army officer what would become of her children if the slaves were freed, a poor white mountain farmer, in a blue uniform also, gave prophetic advice when he remarked, "Put them chaps in the truck patch." Because that is exactly what happened. And Bailey takes us into the field and garden with her after the war when the slaves are gone.

Another question social historians have about antebellum life in the master's house is, "Where did they all sleep?" Sylvan Home was a big house, but altogether it had only six rooms, halls upstairs and down, and a separate kitchen. Bailey's account tells us that the smaller children slept in the master bedroom. Figure 4 drawn by Neill McCaskill, a great-grandson of Charles Bullock who owned Sylvan Home when it burned in 1966, shows, according to family tradition, that the boys slept in one upstairs bedroom, the girls in the other. The only access to the girls' room is a stair up from the master bedroom. The reader thinks immediately that Charles Bullock was a man who knew how to keep an eye on his daughters! Yet another house in the neighborhood, the Nathan Strong House, built ten or twelve years earlier, had the same arrangement. Was the custom peculiar to this community or common at the time and simply never mentioned?

Charles Bullock seems to have seen his role vis à vis his children, as well as his slaves, as that of benevolent dictator. Sister Nannie was at least forty at the time Bailey recounts that she interceded to get their father to permit her older sister to go to a camp meeting, and he did not even feel compelled to explain his reluctance to give permission.

Another area touched by this memoir is the home front during the Civil War. We are told how independent the Bullock plantation had become by 1861, that it provided everything from the cloth to be made into clothing to the dye with which to color it. This, and the fact that the plantation was not on a main road, probably kept the annoyance of the military presence to a minimum, although contents of the Bullock smokehouse and their livestock were taken by both armies. The map in figure 5 shows where the Bullock place lay in relation to the fighting that went on in connection with General Frederick Steele's Camden Expedition.

Bailey reveals details about the plantation's household economy, medical practices, and religion as she takes us into the kitchen, the slave nursery, and the church.

Finally, this document is useful for the light it sheds on certain aspects of Arkansas history. Perhaps in no other southern state is the culture as deeply divided by the rift between the two dominant patterns of southern culture, "hill" and "plantation." In the minds of most outsiders, including those of historians, the hill model dominates the vision of Arkansas culture. The truth, as this memoir illustrates, is that there has always been a deep vein of plantation culture in Arkansas, not only along the eastern edge, in the Delta, but in pockets elsewhere, wherever there was enough flat, fertile ground amenable to cotton and the plantation system it took to raise it profitably. The plantation life described here is as much a part of the cultural history of Arkansas as that of the more publicized hill regions.

The Family

Bailey's father, Charles Lewis Bullock (1811–1886) was a member of a large and distinguished planter family in Warren County (now Vance County), North Carolina, the ninth of eleven children born to James and Nancy Bullock. He married Sara Jane Shapard (or Shepard) (1813–1852) and they moved in 1835 or 1836 to Fayette County, in western Tennessee, where Mr. Bullock operated a successful plantation near

Dancyville. In 1848 or 1849, according to Bailey's account, they started for Texas with the families of Kimbrough Jones, Alexander Littlejohn, and Jesse R. Harris.

While still in North Carolina Charles and Sara Bullock had a daughter, Fanny Lyne, "Sister Fannie," who married Thomas L. Dickinson and lived in Tennessee. After their move to Tennessee, they had Nancy (1836–1907), "Sis Nannie," who never married and who virtually raised the younger children in the Bullock family; Sara Catherine, "Sister Kate," who married Samuel L. Taylor in 1861 and remained in Tennessee; Mary Helen, who married Homer Cross and went to live in nearby Hempstead County; Thomas Shapard, "Brother Tom," who married Mary E. Barcus and lived at Sylvan Home until his death in 1876, following a fall from his horse; Arianna Booker, "Sister Anna Booker," who married Dr. Horace Palmer in 1863; Kimbrough, "Brother Kim," who died of a fever while on duty with the Confederate Army; and Susan Yancey (1847–1883), "Sue," or "Honey," who did not marry.

After the family's arrival in Arkansas, three more daughters were born: Harriet Bailey (1849–1934), the author of these memoirs, who married Nathaniel Beverly Daniel in 1872 and moved with him to his family plantation "Tranquility," near Oxford, North Carolina; Lucy Jane, born in 1851, who died in infancy; and Lucy Agnes, "Lute" born in 1852, who married Dr. Alex McCaskill.

Sara Jane Shapard Bullock died 5 October 1852 and was buried in the Bullock-McCaskill Family Cemetery, referred to by Bailey as "the plum orchard," situated within a couple of hundred feet of the back door of "Sylvan Home," the house Charles Bullock built for his family. Charles then married Mary Wilson Carter in Tennessee, in 1852, and they had five children: James B. (1855–1855), who died in infancy; Martha

Linda (1857–1911), "Mattie," who married Neill McCaskill in 1881 and lived at Sylvan Home; George Wilson (1859–1860), who died in infancy; Charles Lewis Bullock, Jr. (1860–1929), "Charlie," who married Laura Lambeth and then a Miss Emerson; and Cornelia Fletcher Bullock, "Nell," who was born in 1862 and married W. L. Williams in 1886.

Charles Lewis Bullock died in 1886 and Mary Carter Bullock in 1906. They too are buried in "the plum orchard," which is in possession of members of the McCaskill family, descendants of Charles Bullock's daughter Mattie Bullock McCaskill.[4]

The Place: Dallas County, Arkansas, 1848–1872

Sometime in 1848, Charles Bullock packed up his family, slaves, household goods, and farming equipment and with the families of his friends Kimbrough Jones, Jesse R. Harris, and Alexander Littlejohn joined the second leg of The Great Migration—destination Texas. In doing so, he continued to follow the pattern of migration already set: in the 1830s the paths of westward movement led toward Alabama, Tennessee, and Louisiana; by the 1840s the popular destinations had shifted westward to Mississippi, Arkansas, and toward the end of the decade, Texas.[5] The Bullocks, like so many others, took the westward trail twice, and both moves were made at advantageous times. They reached Tennessee just as the cotton boom of the 1830s was getting into high gear and they reached Dallas County, Arkansas, at the beginning of what was probably the most profitable twelve years in its agricultural history. Economically speaking, Charles Bullock was always in the right place at the right time and his success documents some of the reasons why men who were well off where they were would pull up stakes and take their chances in new country.

It may be true, as Bailey recounts, that the settling of the Bullock party in Arkansas was a matter of chance, brought about by the accident that put out one of Charles Bullock's eyes, but it would be difficult to imagine their finding another place with more inducements to stop. For the Manchester area of Dallas County, Arkansas, had already been settled by people from Fayette County, Tennessee, who were undoubtedly well known to Charles Bullock, as well as to the other members of the party. Indeed, some of the greatest speculation in land in the Manchester area was done by The Somerville Land Company, formed in Fayette County, Tennessee, on 14 February 1836.[6] Included among the founders of this land company was Kimbrough Jones' brother, Nathaniel K. Jones, who may have arrived in Dallas County before the Bullock party, although he had sold his interest in the land company in 1839. Thomas C. Hudson, who showed Charles Bullock around with a view to selling him land, was agent and attorney for A. R. Govan, principal shareholder of this company.[7]

Dallas County was formed 1 January 1845 from parts of Bradley and Clark Counties. Manchester Township, where the Bullock party settled, was created in 1836 in Clark county and was part of the area taken from Clark County to form Dallas County. In 1869, part of Manchester Township, including the land owned by members of the Bullock party, was reannexed by Clark County.[8] So Bailey Bullock Daniel was born in Dallas County, but by the time she left Arkansas in 1872, Sylvan Home, the Bullock family plantation, was again in Clark County where it remains to this day. The rate of growth for this area may be roughly gauged by comparing a few figures for 1845 with those for 1859. At that time, property was assessed at about half its actual value.

> In 1845, Dallas County had 217 polls; 52,529 acres of land were assessed at $156,776; 428 slaves were assessed at $163,250; there were two pleasure carriages. In 1859, there were 815 polls; 232,171 acres of land were assessed at $863,944; 2,341 slaves were assessed at $1,695,950; and there were 114 pleasure carriages.[9]

The Bullock party was, in itself, a traveling community consisting of more than a hundred people, including twenty-seven or so white family members and about eighty slaves. Among them, the four families owned a total of eighty-one slaves in 1849, according to the 1850 census slave schedule. In Dallas County they found a settled community of familiar, like-minded people who wanted to establish the same kind of society they had set out to build for themselves. In fact, for many of those already there, this was the second leg of the westward migration which had begun, like the Bullocks', in North Carolina. Surely the new emigrants found comfort in the fact that while the religious and educational institutions they required were not yet in place, with familiar neighbors like these to help, it would not be difficult to establish them. The customs, folkways, and social expectations they had transported from North Carolina to Tennessee should be easier to establish in Arkansas among neighbors with the same values and memories. "Southern" culture implied differences in rank, and Bailey gives hints occasionally about the attention paid to this sort of thing. While some families surely went west in the hopes of rising on the social scale, the Bullocks and their friends were already at the top of the ladder and knew it. Their vision of a new world did not involve changing the social ways of the old; societal expectations were not abandoned when they moved but were brought along and tended like cherished plants.

This is perhaps different from the situation they might have found in Texas and marks one of the differences between Arkansas culture in the plantation areas, which is "southern" in nature, and the "western" culture that grew in Oklahoma and Texas, just a short distance farther west. Venable Daniel, who later became Bailey Bullock Daniel's brother-in-law, went to Texas immediately after the Civil War and wrote back to the family in North Carolina about his surprise at the egalitarian ways in Texas. He begins by saying that he feels that he has arrived in a strange, new country and then explains why.

> McKinney Texas
> Sept. 28th 1866

> . . . There is less attention paid here to the gradation of society than any where I have ever been. There seems nothing here to form an aristocracy: if a man gives a party here everybody comes without an invitation except the ladies are generally invited. The daughter of the Governor will dance at a party with a shoe maker, a house carpenter or a merchant alike. Governor Throckmorton the recent gov. elect lives three miles from here: every one calls him "Jim" from the ox driver to the lawyer.[10]

Things were not quite as socially relaxed in plantation areas of Arkansas where the soil for southern culture was as rich as the ground they bought to plant cotton in, which was, indeed, fertile, plentiful, and cheap.

The reasons for migrating were no doubt as complex as recent scholarly opinion surmises, but one thing is certain, it took capital, a sense of adventure, and the dream of betterment to make the removal of an operation the size of Bullock's feasible.[11] He had a wife and eight children, about forty slaves, furniture, and the household equipment required for such a large group, as well as the farming implements necessary for clearing ground and starting up a farm. The dispatch with which Mr. Bullock faced the challenges of the frontier can be seen in the speed with which he housed his dependents and put his land into production.

Bailey relates that not one acre of the land her father purchased on arrival in Arkansas had been cleared. Surely the success with which ground was cleared and crops planted is a tribute, not only to the master whose vision led them all there, but to the slaves who provided the labor to clear, within two years, enough virgin forest to produce the crops listed below in the census for 1850. It must be remembered that the work was done with elementary tools, and crops were undoubtedly planted among tree stumps. Yet by any standards, the Bullock plantation began producing immediately. They probably arrived in 1848; the 1850 census records, which reflect the farm production in 1849, show these assets:

> Improved land: 200 acres; Unimproved land: 440 acres; cash value of farm: $4200.; Value of implements: $150.; 5 horses, 4 asses or mules, 5 milk cows, 6 working oxen, 10 other cows; value of livestock: $800.; Farm produce: 950 bushels corn, 50 bushels oats, 20 bales ginned cotton (400 lb. bales), 40 bushels peas and beans, 400 bushels sweet potatoes, 70 lbs. butter. According to the slave schedule, he had 34 slaves.[12]

By the time the 1860 census was taken, he had almost tripled his land holdings, his cotton production had increased tenfold, and the farm was capable of sustaining itself, as it would have ample opportunity to prove between 1861 and 1865. The production figures in the 1860 census apply, of course, to the 1859 crop.

> Improved land: 550 acres; unimproved land: 1200 acres; value of land: $7,000; value of implements: $520; 4 horses, 14 asses and mules; 14 milk cows; 8 working oxen; 25 other cows; 50 sheep; 100 swine; value of livestock: $2100.; 250 bushels wheat; 56 bushels rye; 4000 bushels corn; 281 bales ginned cotton (400 lb. bales); 100 lbs. wool; 200 bushels peas and beans; 450 bushels sweet potatoes; 300 lbs. butter; 6 tons hay; value of homemade manufactures: $100.; value of slaughtered animals: $200.

According to the slave schedule he had 51 slaves.[13]

The land on which Charles Bullock built his family's home, a 239 acre plot bought from Pleasant Ward of Fayette County, Tennessee, on 29 October 1849, cost him $599.37—$2.51 an acre.[14] And the soil was certainly hospitable to cotton. Without knowing exactly how many acres he planted in cotton in 1860, it is impossible to compute his bales-per-acre yield, but the 281 ginned bales he listed for 1860, in addition to the other listed produce, on a farm with only 550 improved acres, represented an impressive achievement. It was much better than the Dallas County average of 137.6 ginned bales on farms of comparable size, those with 501–750 improved acres.[15]

From a financial point of view, 1848 was an opportune time for Charles Bullock to arrive in Dallas County, prepared as he was to go immediately into cotton production. Cotton prices were rising through the 1850s and Dallas County's production rose even faster than the average for Arkansas, which was impressive in comparison to other southern states. The annual Arkansas cotton production for the period 1850–51 was 69,956 bales; for the period 1860–61, 262,531 bales. Dallas

County's production was 1556 bales in 1850; 9,229 bales in 1860. The rate at which land was put into production during this decade was as impressive as the increased yield of farmland. In 1850 there were 24,065 acres of improved land in Dallas County; in 1860, 50,786 acres.[16]

By the end of 1852 Charles Bullock had built houses for his slaves and a mansion for his family that stood until 1966 when it was lost to fire. Bailey relates that it was built to withstand hurricanes. Charles Bullock's great-grandson, Neill McCaskill, who renovated the building in the 1940s, gives an idea here of the solidity of this structure:

> When I came to renovate the house I had never seen such construction as this before. The logs were hewn from timber about 16 inches in diameter, approximately 7 inches thick by 16 inches and, of course, notched to fit. I had to jack up the mid-portion of the house where it had settled. I had to move the floor in the hallway—the floor boards in the hallway were one and one half inches thick, random width, pine planking. I knew if I was going to get them back in place I would have to number each board; the boards were sized to fit exactly where they were nailed on the floor joists, which were round logs and uneven. There was wainscoting thirty inches high in the hallway. It was difficult because they had to use shims with small wedges in order to make the walls plumb over the rough surfaces on the logs.[17]

We are fortunate to have photographs of Sylvan Home, Neill McCaskill's drawing of the original house plan, his site plans of the farm buildings around the main house as well as the site plan by Bailey that shows the situation of the barns, office, gin, and slave quarters of the house servants in relation to the main house. (See figures 1 to 4.)

Charles Bullock's business sense, demonstrated by his

success during his first ten years on the frontier, was put to the test by the challenges of war and defeat and again he prevailed. By defying Confederate Government orders to stop planting cotton he was able to hide enough ginned cotton about the place to provide a stake for economic survival after the war. The two hundred bales of cotton he sold at thirty cents a pound after 1865 meant that the Bullocks did not lose everything, as many did. In fact, Mr. Bullock seems to have been in a position to make new investments in Hempstead County as well as in the Palmer Drug Store in Arkadelphia. According to Hempstead County Deed Books he was still buying land there in 1870, which the family owned in 1898, when they donated some of it to a church.

The Text and Sources

The text of this memoir presented an interesting and frustrating editorial challenge. When I agreed to take on the project of editing it, I assumed that the typescript presented to the University of Arkansas Press by Dr. Bailey Webb, Harriet Bailey Bullock Daniel's granddaughter, was the only text there was and therefore my job appeared simple and straightforward: I would identify and document as many people and places as possible from the few scraps of information I could find, make an index, and write an introduction. A textbook case in editing, it seemed like such a quick project that I put aside a larger work that I was supposed to be finishing in order to do this one just for fun. Then the fun began. Dr. Webb sent me the rest of the material: photocopies of about sixty tattered, faded manuscript pages in two different hands; two other typescripts, each slightly different from the one I first saw; and photocopies of some five hundred letters in the Duke University Library written to Bailey Daniel in North Carolina by her family in Arkansas after her marriage and removal in 1872.

The manuscript pages were unattached, unnumbered, and so faded they were barely legible. Dr. Webb had identified the two hands as belonging to her grandmother, Bailey Daniel, and Bailey's daughter, Alice Goodridge Daniel. After sorting them I could see that one manuscript was Bailey Daniel's and the other a transcription of it made by Alice. But Alice's manuscript was not a page for page duplication of Bailey's manuscript; there were some pages in Alice's hand that did not have corresponding pages in Bailey's originals. As for two of the typescripts, apparently Alice copied her mother's manuscript in longhand, then made typescripts to be given to other members of the family, but these differed slightly, one having a few tales in it that the other did not have. There may have been other differences but since part of one typescript had been eaten by rats, it is impossible to be sure. The third typescript, which was the first one I saw, had been made by Dr. Webb by splicing the other two.

My first thought was that I would use Bailey Daniel's manuscript for my text, because it was, after all, what she had written. Her daughter, as any good teacher would do, had tidied the text—regularized the spelling and punctuation, first in longhand, then in the typescripts. But there simply was not enough of Bailey's original text to make using it feasible, and a comparison of the remaining scraps in both hands indicated that Alice followed her mother's text pretty closely and consistently in the matter of meaning. Where there are differences between those scraps and the typescripts, it must be remembered that Alice left an account of the way in which she had encouraged her mother to write these things down, and it is significant that she promised to help her mother by *writing for her* when her mother got tired. Most probably, Alice made the typescripts in consultation with her mother. They differ in phrasing from the extant segments of the manuscripts, but not in the general sense of things. It must be remembered that Bailey Daniel wrote this memoir episodically, and the *order* of the episodes was left to the family editors, Alice Goodridge Daniel and Bailey Webb.

Dr. Bailey Webb did a fine job of splicing the two typescripts to make a composite and I ended up using her text, as I had originally planned to do, referring to the manuscripts for clarification. There were two places where it seemed to me that there was a genuine difference between typescript and manuscript readings and in both cases I took the manuscript's reading, enclosed it in brackets and explained my reasoning in a note. I included a few sentences from the manuscripts that were not in any of the typescripts and enclosed them in brackets also. I made one other change. The typescripts all use quotation marks around "uncle" and "aunt" when they refer to black people; Bailey Daniel's manuscript does not. Since it is obvious from the context of this memoir that these are the customary titles of respect for black people in the place and time in which they were written, I have removed the quotation marks.

As for sources, in the beginning I thought it unlikely that there would be much information about the region on the Ouachita River where the Bullock party settled; I doubted that I would even be able to find exactly where Sylvan Home had been situated. After all, Tulip and Princeton, thriving towns when Bailey Daniel was a girl, have virtually disappeared. Wrong again, I was delighted to find that in the winter of 1979–80, The Clark County Historical Association had devoted a special edition of *The Clark County Historical Journal* to the Manchester Community that revealed more context for the Daniel manuscript than I would have dreamed it possible to find and that I certainly could not have dug up myself in fewer than five years, if at all. The "little" project that had looked so interesting to do because there was so little to it was suddenly a major undertaking with more secondary material than is usually available for writing local Arkansas history. One of the most interesting and useful surprises was an M. A. thesis in anthropology, written by Sharon Luvois Shugart at the University of Arkansas in 1990, based on records kept by her great-grandfather, H. F. Shugart, who owned a plantation in nearby Owen Township at the time Charles Bullock was starting his. "A Socioeconomic Analysis Of A Small Plantation in Dallas County, Arkansas 1844–1868," provides a wealth of information about running a frontier plantation with an analysis of that particular plantation's production in relation to the rest of Dallas County and Arkansas. And finally, not only was it easy to find the site of the Bullock plantation, I found a descendant of Charles Bullock living on it, within ten feet of the site of Sylvan Home. I was taken there to meet Neill McCaskill, the owner, by his sister Clara McCaskill and brother Claude, the grandchildren of Bailey Bullock Daniel's younger sister Mattie. We went together to "the plum orchard," the Bullock-McCaskill family cemetery behind the house, where Charles and his two wives Sara and Mary, as well as other members of the family are buried. The McCaskills were kind enough to provide me with photographs of the family and house, a site plan, and a plan of the original house.

A Remembrance of Eden

1

Your grandpa, Charles Bullock, was born in Warren County, North Carolina, February 26, 1811. I remember little of what he may have told us about his early life, but there are some things I heard my elders say which made a lasting impression upon my mind.

Under the care of his parents, he grew up with three sisters and eight brothers on a large plantation, tilled by slaves, and enjoyed the social life of a wealthy, aristocratic community. His father and mother, James and Nancy Bullock, never joined any church, though the latter was a baptized member of the Episcopal Church, and her generation called her blessed.

Your Great-grandpa was a worldly-minded, card-playing man. Early one morning Grandma met him at the door as he was returning from an all-night game to give orders to his slaves before going to another party.

"Mr. Bullock," she said quietly, "money spent at one card party would raise two children." He remained at home that day and never attended another party.

I remember Pa's sister Nancy said that her mother would never allow the children to gather blackberries on Sunday, and gave them as a reason that only common people and Negroes gather fruit on that day.

When your Grandpa was eighteen years old, he went in company with some neighbors to sell a load of tobacco in Clarksville, Virginia. The weather was chilly, and when they stopped to camp for the night, he took a drink of whiskey proffered him by another member of the party. This was his first and last. The memory of it served as a life-long warning.

Two of your Grandpa's associates when he was a young man were his cousins, Susan and Agnes Bullock, and through them, perhaps, he was led to join Nutbush Presbyterian Church, now of Vance County, North Carolina. At one time it was thought that he and Agnes would be married, and the family was disappointed when she married William Hare, and left your Grandpa to seek a wife elsewhere.

He did not lose much time grieving over his lost love, for he was about twenty-one when he married Sarah Jane Shapherd. She chanced to be his partner for pulling candy at a party, and so beautiful a one she proved, he sought and won her as his partner for life. On January the 29th, 1833, they were married at the home of her father, Thomas Shapherd, of Person County, North Carolina. She was a decided Methodist and her ancestors were from Virginia. Neither his nor her family, it seems, approved of the marriage, but it was a most devoted couple, and they lived with his mother until after the birth of their little daughter, Fanny Lyne, in 1834.

Shortly after their marriage, Grandpa Shapherd must have moved to Fayette County, Tennessee, for some time in eighteen and thirty-five or thirty-six, Pa followed him there with his family. Mounted upon his favorite horse, accompanied by Mother, the baby, and Aunt Arianna Shapherd Webb, Mother's sister, all snugly tucked in one covered wagon, and his household furniture in another, also followed by a line of steer wagons bearing the slaves and their belongings, he set out across the hills to join the other emigrants going west. The slow procession made its way along the rough roads of the hill country to the still more rugged mountain passes and on out to western Tennessee. I remember Pa said they stopped a few days with Mother's Uncle Robert Shapherd, who lived in Chattanooga, Tennessee.

On reaching Fayette County, he bought a plantation a few miles from Dancyville, and settled near Grandpa Tom Shapherd. There the family lived for several years, when Pa again joined a party of emigrants bound for Texas. There were now six daughters and two sons in the home. He said he had too many girls to live in Tennessee.

Mr. Kimbrough Jones[18] and Mr. Jesse Harris[19] agreed to go too. In the aristocratic Jones family were Mary, Anna and Calvin; in the clever unassuming Harris family were Betty, Bill, Sue and Patty; and in our family were Fanny, Nannie, Kate, Mary Helen, Anna Booker, Sue, Tom and Kim. I think Mr. Alex Littlejohn[20] of Oxford, North Carolina, was Pa's most intimate friend in the party. Again packing their wives, children and infirm colored people in wagons with their belongings, and leaving the strong slaves to go by foot, they set out to cross the Mississippi bottoms, enroute to the storied land of Texas.

Aunt Rose, our black mammy, said she was just a slip of a girl and when Pa left Tennessee he sold some of his slaves. Among them was Aunt Lucy, the mother of the two boys, Shadrack and Damon, whom he wanted to carry to Texas. Damon was not two, and Shadrack was older. Aunt Lucy was sold after the wagons were ready to start. Shadrack had been seated in the wagon with other little Negro boys, and Pa told Aunt Rose to take the baby Damon from Aunt Lucy and get on the wagon as it moved off. Aunt Rose said she was just a stripling, but she could never forget that day. Aunt Lucy, the mother, ran just as fast as she could behind the wagon, screaming, "Oh, my chillun! Give me my baby. Give me my baby!" Blinded by grief and heedless of her step, she fell. The wagon rolled on and Aunt Rose always looked after the two motherless boys, and they were favorites on the plantation.[21]

Sister Mary Helen told me much about the journey which has been forgotten. I cannot remember how long they traveled, but she said the children had much fun on the way. The first night they were in the pines they thought it was raining, but raising the tent cover, they saw the moon shining, the trees bowing, and heard the mourning of the wind passing through the pines.

She said once the party stopped at a little log cabin; from it came a woman poorly dressed and wearing a faded calico bonnet. With her was a pretty little girl who jumped on the wagon wheel to see the children. The mother screamed out, "Git down from thar, you heifer, you!" And she "got."

At another cabin they heard this snatch of quarrel, "Mammy, Mammy, Sally takes two sops out de deep sop while I takes one out de shaller." They stopped at another home where a woman drawled in long nasal tones in reply to one of her children who addressed her, "Jane, what makes yer talk ser long? I don't talk long, and yer pappy, he don't talk long. I can't see whar yer git yer long talk frum."

While the emigrants were camping on the banks of the Ouachita River in Arkansas, Pa hurt his eye with the spring of a clock he was trying to repair. The injury was so serious that the party lingered in camp while he sent to Camden, forty miles away, for a doctor. He could never again see out of that eye, and ere it was well enough for him to resume the journey, he looked favorably upon the Ouachita Valley, and decided to go no further west.

Mr. Tommy Hudson[22] and Mr. Nathan Strong[23] warmly welcomed the emigrants as new neighbors, and I guess advised about the purchase of land. That part of the state had been laid off into sections, every other one of which had been retained by the government for the benefit of schools and railroads. "Uncle Tommy," as Mr. Hudson was called, sold land to Mr. Kim Jones. Mr. Harris bought four miles away, across the L'au Frais River, and Pa bought a farm on which was a small two room log house, with stick chimneys and with wooden shutters for windows.[24] There was a shelter in front, and another behind the house. I say shelter, and not porch, for when I visited the place after I was grown, I remember the posts of the shelters were set in the ground, and flat rocks were used for floors.

There our family lived for more than a year, and there I was born on December the eighteenth, eighteen and forty-nine. When I, Pa's seventh daughter arrived, he was sore troubled, but Mother said they should be glad and thankful none of the children were deformed, and that all were good looking and showed plenty of sense, and that I was a pretty, sprightly little thing. Moreover, there were two fine, well-grown boys to perpetuate the Bullock name. They say the year I was born there was a freshet in the Ouachita Valley, and if there had been bridges across the creeks they were washed away, and if mills were operating, we could not reach them for grain, nor could we get anywhere to buy meal or flour. For nearly a month fifty or sixty lived on corn hominy and parched corn.

Pa either bought or entered two thousand acres of land, and at the time of his settlement there was not as much as an acre of it cleared. He sold the plantation on which I was born to Mr. Daniel Jones, an uncle of J. K. Jones, afterwards congressman from Arkansas, and moved to a new purchase several miles away.[25] There he built a large two-room comfortable house, with a jump above, and a shed the length of the house at the back. This was for a permanent weaving room and a kitchen, but we lived in it until Pa could build our dwelling house. There were also cabins for the Negro quarters, stables, barns, cribs, a gin house, and other houses to build.

Our dwelling house was a frame building of six large rooms, two wide halls, dressing-rooms and closets. Not long before the dwelling was built, a hurricane had swept over that part of Arkansas, which caused Pa to exercise great care in constructing a house, fitted to stand in time of storm. I was told that he built the front rooms of hewn logs, six by eight inches, which were dovetailed together, and then strips were put on with large wooden pegs, before the house was ceiled and weatherboarded. I know the house was not more than twelve inches from the ground, for I could crawl under it in only a few places. It had wide glass windows with small panes. The top of the house was of shingles, and the floors were of dressed plank. The outside of the house was painted white; some of the rooms were light blue or dove colored.[26]

The Negro cabins were built of smaller logs, chinked and daubed, and had puncheon floors, stick chimneys, wooden shutters for windows, and they were covered with split boards. The shutters of the windows had to be kept open, even on the coldest days, to admit light.

[I don't think there was but one painted house between the river and Tulip.] When Sue and I were little girls we dressed up and went over there to have our daguerreotypes taken. We thought it was the finest place in the world, with its green blinds and plastered rooms, and there was a piano in the parlor. Why such rich people should let their boys cut wood and work in the fields was a mystery to us. Our brothers never did. Our people thought that if their sons had to control the slaves, it was best that they should not work with them before they were grown.[27]

Game was plentiful. One day soon after our arrival in this new country, our cook stepped out in the yard and killed a wild turkey with a stick. Deer frequented the surrounding forests; once Mr. Jones stood in his tracks and killed eight. I remember there was a pyramid of deer horns in Mr. Jones's yard eight or ten feet high. Pa built a seat up in a tree near the "salt licks" and here he would sit to kill deer as they came to get salt.

Now and then "Uncle" Tommy Hudson would bring us a treat of bear meat. I was told that one night a bear came and took a pig from the pens near the house, and we could some-times hear wolves howling in the distance. Once Mr. Jones brought us a beaver's tail—a dish of rare delicacy.

In a few years the Negro slaves on the plantation were numerous. Most of them were inherited or raised; few were bought. All of us were required to be courteous and respectful to them, and to treat them with due and proper consideration. We had to call the male grown-ups "uncle" and the females "aunt." Even before our dwelling was completed, the cabins down at the quarters had to be built. They were comfortable houses, with a garden in the back and a small yard in front. The "Quarters" were on the east of our house, and somewhat back.[28]

My mother's maid was Moriah—Aunt 'Riah we called her. Back east in North Carolina she had married a slave who was not given with her to my mother when the latter was married. They had two children, Polly and Jenny. When Pa went West Aunt 'Riah had to leave her husband John, but she took her two children with her, for the law in that state gave the chil-dren to the slave mother separated from her husband.

Uncle Billy's wife belonged to Pa's brother Robert Bullock in North Carolina, and he had to leave his wife and children to follow "Marster" as foreman of the plow hands. Uncle Billy and Aunt 'Riah afterwards married each other, and were perhaps the most highly esteemed of all of our slaves; they surely had more privileges. After a time Aunt 'Riah became the cook and held that position until the close of the war. Polly was scullion help; Emily and Leah served in the house. 'Liza was generally my nurse and after I was grown she let me know how much trouble she had keeping up with me and making me wear my bonnet. Aunt Rose was our black mammy. Uncle John W. was Aunt Rose's husband, but belonged to Colonel Boseman, who lived across the river. For years he would come to see Aunt Rose every other week, besides spending Christmas and big-meeting times with her, but later married one of Colonel Boseman's slaves and left Aunt Rose a widow. She grieved much for a time, but years later, just before the close of the war, she married a right young Negro who lived near.

[Aunt Rachel's husband was Uncle Fed who led the hoe hands. Once Sister Nannie walked in her sleep and seeing a light through the crack in their door, went quietly in and sat by the fire. Uncle Fed, on seeing her, said "Rachel, Rachel wake up. There's an angel in the corner," and he would not move till Rachel found it was only one of the white "chilluns" and carried her to the house.]

I always liked to write and after I was seventy-five amused myself living over the days back home and enrolling the names of our slaves in the following lines. I might have made some early attempt at writing, but Sister Nannie, who for the most part raised me, discouraged my efforts, saying she had no use for women writers.

Slaves at Sylvan Home

Shall I ever forget colored friends of the past?
Will Time blur their faces, fly ever so fast?
Uncle Billy, Pa's foreman, followed the plow.
Uncle Fed, his brother, led the hands with the hoe.
Uncle Oscar we loved dearly; he oft let us ride;
Behind his fat oxen from the white folks we'd hide.
There were Damon and Shadrack, Harry, Dick, Phil,
Who were older, not younger, than Henry and Bill.
June was the smithy, and ever gave trouble
'til he swam in the river and sank with a bubble.
Macklin, our coachman, was handsome and tall;
He made all our shoes with needle and awl.
Edmund and Jerry, good riders were they,
When the "Yanks" got our horses, they rode them away.
Now came Robert and Kemp, with Dan, called "Tuck,"
With Sam and Charles Lewis named for "Marster" and luck.
Aunt Lizzy and Patsy were sisters so good,
They gave children pleasure whenever they could.
Aunt Rose was black Mammy: I sat on her knees
And heard her tell stories of rabbits and bees.
She, with her Sis Rachel were black to behold,
But their hearts were as bright and as pure as gold.
Aunt 'Riah was cook, and we all understood
She prepared for us children the very best food.
Aunt Clay spun coarse warp, and oft would depend
On my reeling her thread, the task to soon end.
Aunt Fanny was milker; with pigeen so bright
She went to the cowpen each morning and night.
While I am digressing, Time does not tarry;
I hasten to name the girls I saw marry:
Matilda, Rebecca, Priscilla, and Grace
Betsy, Pollyanna, Eliza, apace
Jenny and Martha married after the war;

I had ever known Jerry, but Sam never saw.
Hannah and Cat, Ceily and 'Line
Pretended a husband they never could find.
There were Harriet, Betsy Ann, Letty and Vick,
Emily and Leah, cousins of Dick.
Victoria, Nelly, Lucy, Eva, and Joe,
With Tiny and Delia, are all that I know.[29]

Our overseer was Mr. Joe Hinton Scott from North Carolina.[30] They told me he had been engaged to be married to a girl in that state, but when the day appointed for the marriage came, his heart failed him and instead of going to claim his bride, he took the fork of the road leading from her home and out to the unknown West. It was in Tennessee that Pa employed him to be his overseer. He seldom spoke of his life back East.

Though he was always kind to us, when under the influence of whiskey, he was at times cruel to the Negroes. He then evaded members of our family. Once when he was drunk he got mad with a Negro man, and pulled a lock of his hair out by the roots. Again, he whipped some of the women until the clothes on their backs were clotted with blood. I saw it myself. Yet, when Mr. Scott was not under the influence of whiskey, he was a kind master and a good overseer.

His place was no easy one to fill. The Negroes, often misunderstanding and misunderstood, were sullen and rebellious. Tiny, one of the slaves, told me that once when Uncle Fed resisted Mr. Scott, who started to punish him for some misdemeanor, the latter drew out his knife and cut the Negro across the stomach, inflicting such a wound he had to be taken to the doctor to have it sewed up. Mr. Scott was deeply grieved, and said he did this in self defense for he was afraid of the angry Negro. The other slaves did not seem to blame Mr. Scott.

I tell you these things to show you why I was always a rank

abolitionist in a section and time when slavery was popular.

As I have said, Pa was a strong Presbyterian but Mother was a great Methodist, as were all the folks I knew, except Mr. and Mrs. Trigg, who lived four miles away, over the river. Pa attended the Methodist church regularly while he lived in Tennessee and when he reached Arkansas, joined Manchester Church of that denomination until he could "do better," as he said. The one room building of log was about two miles from home and Pa's friend Mr. Littlejohn was the pastor. Later, when some of Pa's former acquaintances came into the new country and settled across the L'au Frais River, Pa helped them build a nice framed house for a church. It was called Bethlehem, and here he and his family united and started a Methodist Sunday School. It was years later that the true reason for Pa's leaving Manchester was known to us; he and Mr. Littlejohn fell out about some harness Pa bought for Mr. Littlejohn on one of his trips to New Orleans. They said Mr. Littlejohn was high-tempered. Pa was.

Attending this church was a family of very poor but intelligent girls that Mother loved dearly. Their father carried his Webster's Blue Back speller to Sunday School where he soon learned to read and became a useful member of our church. The mother did weaving for us. All five of the daughters became women of worth and some of them married into families of some prominence in that section of the state. Night and morning Pa had family prayers, and all the servants of the house were required to attend if possible. We memorized passages from the Bible and favorite hymns on Sundays.

Mother's great desire was that her children should be educated. When our family moved to Arkansas Sister Fanny remained at school in Tennessee, the other older children were sent either to Tulip or to Arkadelphia, and the younger ones attended the day school near home.

After the little ones had been going to school a while, Mr. Baugh, the teacher, told them if they did not bring ink to school the next day he would whip them. When they related their trouble to Mother, she said that no one had time to go eight miles for a bottle of ink and they must tell their teacher so.

The next morning the children started out as usual, walked the road as long as they were in sight of the house, then turned into the woods, built a playhouse, ate lunch, and returned home at the usual hour. This truancy kept up through the week. On Sunday at church, Mother inquired of Mr. Baugh how the children were getting on at school, and he replied they had not been for nearly a week. Mother, guessing the trouble, told him she supposed they were afraid to go without ink, as they said he had threatened to whip them.

"I did not mean to whip them," he said, "I just thought I could squeeze a little ink out of them by the threat." The children returned to school the next day unwhipped.

After Mr. Baugh stopped teaching, the settlers procured the services of a Yankee, Mr. Gilky. He was bald-headed and had a smooth face and pleasant smile. He played the fiddle, wrote poetry and painted pictures with oil colors.

In school he was very strict with the children, and believed that forgetfulness was a sin and stubbornness a crime. When Brother Tom went to school without his books, he was whipped and sent home for them; and when "Honey" (Sister Sue) did not mind, he tried to conquer her with the rod. I was told that he whipped her until the blood streamed down her legs. He said she was stubborn, but I know she was dull. The younger children disliked Mr. Gilky, but the older ones were fond of him. He was partial to Sister Kate and perhaps it was through his unconscious influence that she formed the resolve to herself to become a teacher.

2

The name of our new place was "Sylvan Home." Soon after we moved from the "shack" to the two-room house Pa had built for the kitchen, a little Lucy came, and left us when but a few weeks old. Hers was the first grave in the plum orchard back of the garden. In time another little sister was born into our home and they named her "Lucy" also. We called her "Lute."

Aunt 'Riah told me that when Lute was about two months old, Mother rode horseback behind Pa some distance to see a sick child, whom she nursed until the spirit left the body, then prepared it for burial. Soon after that Mother herself was taken sick and when she was strong enough to walk around, suffered all the time with a pain in her side. In the fall of the year she became critically ill and all the children away at school were called home. After a few days of intense suffering, God took her and her body was laid by that of her little babe in the plum orchard.

I cannot remember my mother and we did not have a picture of her. The neighbors said she was pretty and never grew old. She was often taken for Pa's daughter, though he was only two years her senior. Aunt 'Riah said she was active, though she always walked with a stick. The years of pioneer life would have taxed the strength of one more lusty and less tenderly bred. Rearing the children, managing the servants, and planning the new home were tasks far too great for her frail body. Besides, she was known throughout the section as being a good nurse and cheerfully responded to calls made by the needy and suffering throughout the community. Neighbors were neighborly in those times.

I do not think Mother lived to enjoy the new house in its completion, for Mr. Dan Pryor from Tulip was, at the time of her death, staying with us and working on the new building. He said her coffin was the prettiest he had ever made. It was covered with black silk velvet and lined with white silk.

Though but three years old, I have a faint recollection of Mother's burial. My old nurse "Cat," standing by the yellow peach tree at the head of her grave, held me in her arms. I saw some men, bearing a long box, come slowly from the house. Everyone was crying or looking as if he wished to. The men set the black box on blocks near a hole in the ground, then placed underneath the box two leather straps by which they lowered it into the hole. The straps made a fearful creaking sound as the men drew them out. Then some planks were laid over the box and men threw in dirt, with an awful noise, until the hole was filled and a mound raised above. The grown folks said I could not remember this but when I told about being in "Cat's" arms by the yellow peach tree, they no longer doubted.

Cat said that before Mother died she told her to bring me to her bedside and placing her hand on my head, she said, "Meet me in heaven, my child; and may God help you." She asked a neighbor, Mrs. Harris, to take the baby Lute to her home and care for her, for she would love her.

Mother left eight daughters and two sons. Sister Nannie, the second daughter, said she asked her to care for the motherless little ones of the home and this charge Sister Nannie ever faithfully kept; though at first Sister Fanny took Mother's place as mistress of the home and Sister Nannie returned to school in Sommerville with some of the other sisters.

Pa's grief was terrible. Aunt 'Riah said that after the funeral was over and all the folks gone, Pa went off alone and lay on a log near the branch in front of the house. He stayed there a long time, until they all got worried about him. Uncle Billy finally went out and sat down by him, but didn't say anything. Just after sundown Pa came to the house, leaning on Uncle Billy's shoulder. Aunt 'Riah said Uncle Billy had had trouble and knew what trouble "Marster" was in, and it almost broke his heart to see him that way.

It had been a servant's task at night to see that we had our supper of bread and milk, that our faces were washed, our hair brushed, and that we were properly put to bed before dark. But now Pa shared these duties and I remember his tears as he brushed my hair and put on our caps at night. When I rebelled against the maid's washing my face, he would take me on his knee and comfort me.

As Mother had requested, Mrs. Harris took Lute to her house and was really devoted to her. She was the fairest of our family, with her clear rosy complexion, deep blue eyes, and brown hair. The Harrises were not rich, but their home was one of love and ease. All of us liked to stay there, for we were never scolded or blamed, while at home it all seemed so different after Mother went away. Really, Mr. Jesse Harris and his wife were two of the sweetest people I ever saw in my life. Lute soon learned to love them better than she did Pa, who went to see her almost every day and took her gifts to bribe her for her love. Before she was very old, she would run to her foster kin when she saw Pa coming. He said that would never do, so he took her home.

When Pa went on his nightly rounds to see that the doors were locked and the house was safe from fire, he usually sang in low, subdued tones:

> Welcome, welcome, dear Redeemer,
> Welcome to this heart of mine.
> Lord, I make a full surrender;
> All I Have, I give; 'tis Thine-
> Thine entirely, Thine entirely,
> Through eternal ages Thine.

I knew he was missing Mother, too, and when he would return to his seat by the fire, I would creep out of my place in the trundle bed if I were awake (as I often was), and curl up in his lap for sympathy and to sympathize.

Pa more often lost his temper, also, than he did during Mother's life. The servants said she knew how to keep him in a good humor by shielding him from worries and by preparing food which agreed with him. We could usually tell at a glance when he was sick and stood somewhat in awe of him then.

In 1858 Pa, having some financial difficulty with the officers of Bethlehem church and always having been at heart a Presbyterian, went to Arkadelphia, and with nine women organized the first Presbyterian church there. Reverend Beattie, an Irishman, was called to be the pastor. Pa had him come out home once every month when the roads would permit travel and preach to our family and to the slaves. The other members of the family, however, retained their membership at Bethlehem.[31] I never remember going to the Presbyterian Church in Arkadelphia but once before the war.

This church was a small one-room brick structure with a partition through the center dividing men from women. In the rear was an elevated platform provided with four rows of benches for the Negro slaves. The choir occupied the first and second rows of seats in front of the pulpit. Every family had a pew. The charter members of this church were Colonel Charles Bullock, Mrs. Flannagan, Mrs. Witherspoon, Mrs. Cossort, Mr. Morehead, Miss Mary Flow and Miss Nancy Flow.[32] The first pastor was Rev. Alexander Beattie. After his death he was followed by Rev. A. L. Crawford. The people of the church always stood at prayers, while at our church they knelt.

It was while Pa was a widower that a renowned Presbyterian minister from Little Rock visited our home and we three little girls were baptised by him. I remember that Sunday when Pa carried us in the parlor; Lute in his arms, he held me by the hand, and Sue clung to his long black coat-tail. The other members of the family and household servants were gathered around. We were led up to this solemn, dignified stranger with a bowl of water in his hand and were baptised, Pa taking the covenant vows. I do not remember what he said, but it all made a deep impression on me.

Pa was but a man, and nearly a young one, being only forty-two, and he was also pleasure-loving. Soon our neighbors and the servants began to whisper that he was "on the carpet" and, indeed, it was not long before he was courting, the gayest of the gay.

Mr. Jones had a pretty daughter, Miss Mary, who was about Sister Fanny's age, and who now stayed much of the time in our home to keep the latter company. Everything was done to please these two girls. Aunt 'Riah was a splendid cook; Aunt Lizzy, with a few assistants, kept the house pretty much as

Mother had done. Horse-back rides, bird nettings, dinings and parties seemed all the girls thought of.

One night a boy came bearing a note. Some North Carolina kin were visiting at Cousin George Eaton's, ten miles away, and our family was invited to dine there the next day.[33] Before leaving, Sister Fannie made a cake for Aunt 'Riah to bake and told her and Aunt Lizzy to have everything in readiness for the crowd that night. They rode off on horse-back. We little ones were left in the care of Aunt Rose. All day there was a great stir of baking and cleaning going on in the house. About night the crowd came galloping back home and a grand time they all seemed to have, laughing, chatting, singing, and playing, Pa in the midst of them.

Of all the girls, Miss Mary Jones was Pa's favorite. He and Miss Mary would often be seen sitting apart from the others, or strolling along the banks of a nearby stream. Polly and Liza confided to me that "Marster wuz courtin' agin an' wanted to make Miss Mary my Ma." This was not so displeasing to me as one would think, for I liked Miss Mary very much, as she was sweet to all and everything moved along smoothly while she was there.

But one morning, one of our slaves, whose wife lived at Mr. Jones's came up to the house before daylight and called, "Marster, here yer gun. Mars Kim sent it and he say he don't need it no mo'." Sensing trouble, Pa replied, "Set it in the corner, Damon, and go long." Mr. Jones had had one of Pa's guns for years. Soon we learned on hearing of Pa's attention to his daughter, Mr. Jones got "mad as hops" and sent Miss Mary to Sommerville to the same school Sister Nannie and Sister Kate attended. And do you believe it? Sister Kate wrote and thanked Mr. Jones for breaking up the match.[34]

Soon Pa was helping the widow Gibson dismount from her horse at church and was going hunting with Mr. Strong, the widow's father.[35] Then Mr. Jones got over Miss Mary's engagement to Pa (for they really were engaged) and brought us apples, just as he had always done.

Pa next began to write. He had studied Latin and Greek, but men in our family were poor scribes and Pa was no exception. He seldom tarried long with pen in hand and now his taking up so much time with careful composition was a matter of secret wonder and amazement with us. Mail came to Cassamassa, our post office five miles away, only once a week, and now Pa suddenly became very anxious to go for it himself, an errand usually performed by a trusted slave. On one of these weekly rides he took me behind him. I got very tired and the horse's back was the hardest seat I had ever had in my life, but the new experience more than repaid me. The post-office was kept by the merchant in his one room log store. In the front was a porch on which were two big chairs with buckskin bottoms. Furs and hides hung against the wall behind them. I knew these had been traded to the merchant by neighbors for articles in the store. I had never been in a store before, nor seen so many pretty things all at one time. Pa let me buy what I wished and I selected a string of amber-colored glass beads and a gaudy green, yellow and purple piece of cloth for a dress. The merchant gave me a bag of striped candy. That won my heart. On returning home, my sisters laughed at my purchases and I never felt quite as happy and satisfied about them afterwards. They did their shopping in Arkadelphia, eight miles away.

Pa, however, did much of the buying for the family in New Orleans, where he went every fall to sell his cotton. At this time he would buy things for Christmas, for it was near the middle of December, often, when he would return from these trips. The goodies for Christmas would be hidden from us children until time for us to hang up our stockings. I was always prying into things and one Christmas I found the oranges and told the other children where they were. When the grown folks learned this, they told me I should not have one in my stocking and they were as good as their word. I reckon they gave me oranges at other times but not to find one in my stocking was a great punishment—one I could not get over.

After Pa had written and received several letters, he surprised us one day with the announcement that he was going on a visit to his children in school in Sommerville, and to his old friends in the neighborhood where he had lived.

How long he was gone, I do not know. Mr. Scott managed the farm while he was gone and Sister Fanny, as young mistress, had a good time; we children did too, spending perhaps a great part of each day down at the "Quarters."

After a while a letter came that changed the face of everything. Pa and Miss Mary Carter, a young lady who had taught in his home when he lived in Tennessee and who had since been a missionary to the Indians in Indian Territory, were to be married the next week and come straight home.[36]

Poor Sister Fanny! She cried, sang about wanting to go to Mother in heaven, declared that she would never call Miss Mary "Ma," and that she would leave home. She was walking the floor when I went to sleep and was crying when I awoke.

The letter stated, also, that he had bought a new carriage and a pair of mules and that he would bring Sister Nannie home with his bride.

Everything was bustle and hurry at Sylvan Home and in a few days a fine sea-spring carriage, drawn by as handsome a pair of mules as ever I saw, stopped at the front gate. [The Negroes said Pa paid a thousand dollars for this carriage.] The three little girls, Sue, Lute and I ran out to meet Pa and Sister

Nannie. Of course we were delighted to see them. Brother Kim hid behind the big hickory nut tree and peeped out until Pa spied him and brought him forth. I do not remember Brother Tom's greeting, but I know he was always loyal and true to "Ma," as we all, except Sister Fanny, called our step-mother. Sister Fanny and Sister Anna Booker came on behind us, calm and rebellious. Sister Fanny always said "Miss Mary," and soon left home to return some years later a bride.

Ma was thirty and a rather thin, black-eyed, dark-skinned woman, wearing a camel's hair traveling dress and a buff corded bonnet. I thought her pretty. I fear we showed some surprise at the sun-bonnet on the bride, for Sister Nannie remarked, "As our best bonnets kept us from resting on the journey, we put them away and got out our sun-bonnets," which explanation was very kind. I was only five years old but the picture of that meeting never left my mind.

In a few days Sister Fanny said she must finish sewing up the west room carpet. It was a checked, purple and copperas colored rag carpet, woven by a poor neighbor. Ma said she would help whip the seams and soon she and Sister Fanny were at work, chatting pleasantly. When Pa came in later he said, "Dear, you have sewed long enough; let us take a walk." Sister Fanny said, "Yes, I am tired too; let us stop." Pa, who was often hasty, replied, "I said nothing to you. Sew on, and when Moriah comes, give out supper." "Mother always let Moriah get out supper herself," coldly replied Sister Fanny and went to her room.

It seems to me she stayed there most of the time until Mr. Jones took her to the landing where she boarded a boat and went back to Grandpa Shapherd's in Tennessee. There she was married sometime afterward to Mr. Thomas Dickinson, a prosperous merchant of Sommerville.

When Lute was brought home before Pa's marriage, she was allowed to have her own way and was petted and scolded, in turn, by all. She spoke distinctly, memorized verse quickly, and was carried almost daily into the parlor to entertain visitors. There was trouble when Ma came. One day she told Lute to come in the house and she replied, "I shan't," as she continued her play. Ma got two keen little switches and cut her on the feet until she was willing to obey. As they went into the house, Ma laid the switches on the window ledge in the hall, remarking at the same time that they must be put away until she disobeyed again. Then Ma, taking Lute in her lap, told her how she loved her, and how sorry she was about her not minding, until the affectionate, tender-hearted little child went to sleep in her arms.

As soon as Ma closed the door behind her and Lute, Sue and I jumped for the switches, broke them in bits, and flung them away. Afterwards Ma made it clear to us how necessary it was for her to make Lute mind; and I think now, if we three little girls had been left to ourselves, all would have been happier. Sister Anna Booker impressed us with the idea that Ma was nothing before she married Pa, for she brought only one servant with her—only one—and we might know they were "poor white folks."

I was much ashamed of all this afterwards, when I realized how much mistaken we were and how low our prejudice had led us. Ma was truly a splendid woman, of a very fine family. Her people were more opposed to her marriage than we were. Years since, I heard that she stole away from her home, met Pa secretly, mounted behind him on his horse, and rode away to the nearest town to be married. This may, or may not, be true; anyway, her children teased her when they were grown by saying, "Ma, you must have been anxious to get married if you ran away with a one-eyed widower with eleven children." I know Ma was a devoted wife, a kind mistress, and just as good a mother as we would let her be.

Betsy was the name of Ma's maid and she was as good a colored girl as ever I saw. Now we children had never been required to wash our own faces; Lettie did that generally and kept us in good humor. Aunt Rose had to bathe and dress us twice a week. One morning Ma told me to wash my face before coming to breakfast and sent Betsy to see that it was properly done. She went back and told Ma that I did nothing but cry and Ma came out and gave me a whipping. I told her I hated her and wished she were dead; I shall never forget how she cried.

Another time I tried to wash my face alone and could not do it with the basin of water on the shelf where it usually stayed. I took it down and set it on the big chest, full of sheets and pillow-cases. The water could not get through the top to the linen and I never thought of injuring the furniture but Ma, coming out and seeing the water on the lid, slapped me; then I told her that Sister Fanny had said she was nothing before she came there and I believed it now. Again she cried a long, long time and she cried so often after that I expect she wished she had not come to stay.

After a while Ma had a little boy of her own and Pa was surely proud. He named him James for his father. Aunt Patsy said it was "sho bad luck," for every Jim Bullock back east drank or did something mean and we believed her. And I often wondered what Grandpa James Bullock had done to give Aunt Patsy such an impression of his character. However, we all thought the baby fine and Ma gave it to "Honey."

When the baby was old enough to travel, Ma planned a trip back to her home in Tennessee. This was against Pa's judgement, but finally all was arranged and they, with the new baby, started east. Lute and I were sent to Mr. Harris's; Honey to Mr. Hudson's and Sister Nannie, with the aid of the servants, looked after the home and the other children.

How long they stayed in Tennessee I do not know, but I recall when they returned and Uncle Billy came over to Mr. Harris's for Lute and me. He said we had company; Sister Fanny and her husband had come back with Ma and Pa.

I was glad to see Sister Fanny. Mr. Dickinson came to the house some time later with Mr. Scott. We were eating our supper of bread and milk. I was told to kiss Sister Fanny's husband but I refused and kept on eating. After a while I turned to Honey, who had kissed him, and said, "Ain't he ugly?" I was afterwards sharply rebuked by my elders and how I could have said such a thing, I do not know, for he had the sweetest smile and one of the best faces I ever saw.

Baby James grew weaker from day to day and it was not long before another little mound was in the plum orchard and we went about with heavy hearts, for all of us loved the baby.

Mr. Dickinson and Sister Fanny stayed with us for several weeks. Pa and Brother Kim went hunting with him and they killed several deer.

We liked to ramble in the woods and hunt for sweet-gum sap which ran out and hardened in places where the trees had been cut. Ma and Sister Fanny both liked the gum but Pa would never let us chew it in his presence. One evening we were elated when we were given permission to gather some from the trees down on the branch. After much effort, we brought in several chunks of gum, one of which was left in a chair near the fire. When Pa and Mr. Dickinson came in from hunting, Pa took a seat in that very chair. For a while he chatted gaily with the others then started out; the chair followed, hung to the seat of his pants. The grown folks laughed, but we trembled 'til Pa said, "I would whip you but Mary insisted on your getting the stuff for her." We were safe this time.

3

When the Dickinsons returned to Tennessee, they took Sister Anna and Brother Tom with them to go to school. Sister Kate had graduated there and was teaching in Somerville Institute. I learned afterwards that this was Sister Kate's way to help educate her younger sisters and brothers. She boarded with them at Sister Fanny's and had the oversight of their studies.

When the news of Sister Kate's teaching reached the kinfolks back in North Carolina, one of Pa's sisters, your grandmother and my future mother-in-law, said, "I am surprised that Charles would let one of his daughters teach."

As I have said, Mr. Gilky who taught her at home in Arkansas had a great influence over her. After Mother's death, he wrote the following lines, voicing his impression of Sister Kate's childhood and of her beautiful life of service in our home.

> KATIE, when I first beheld thy face
> No sorrow's blight had paled thy youthful brow;
> A mother, then, with love and gentle grace,

Watched o'er thy young days and taught thee how
To meet the cares and wiles of earth; but now
That mother sings the songs of heaven, and wears
A starry crown; yet still with joy, I trow
Looks down to see how well her daughter bears
The weary load of life, O'ercharged with grief and tears.

Thy cheek, I say, was not then paled with grief;
Thy joyous, trusting innocence still but
A charm to life. The autumn's fading leaf,
The forest flowers, the warbling birds seem sent
To glad thy heart, and all their colors blent
To render earth to thee a place of joy:
Thou didst not understand then what sorrow meant;
The bliss of life was all without alloy.
Alas! that envious Time would such sweet peace destroy.

Yet, even then, though happy, thou wast sad—
Not melancholy, as with grief o'ercome,
But looking e'en as if thy spirit had
Pierced through the dim futurity, and from
Its dread revealings thou hadst learned the sum
Of all thy coming care and future woe;
Thy brow was pale with thought and thou wast dumb,
While thy young playmates, prating wondered so
To see thee day by day so sad and silent go.

I wondered, too, and thought it passing strange
That one so young should seem so full of care—
To see a little child forget to range
Through forest, dell, or meadow, smiling fair,
And children's merry sports forget to share;
And seated in some silent nook apart,
Seemed meditating how to best prepare
The inexperienced mind and gentle heart
To act in Life's majestic drama some great part.

And, Oh, how soon He tried thy strength—how soon—
The Master called thee to thy work before
The rising sun had half-way reached its noon.
He sent affliction, terrible and sore:
Yet, thou in meekness all thy suffering bore,
And looked to heaven with firm belief
That He who gave thee strength would grant thee more,
That to thy father's heart, bowed down with grief,
Thou mightest administer the balm, and give relief.

And well, dear Kate, hast thou performed thy part,
And more than daughter's Love and care were thine,
Through trials that had tried the stoutest heart
Thou has gone bravely on, without one sign
Of slightest wish thy duties to resign:
And like a glorious sun beam, bright and warm,
Thou on his darkened pathway still doth shine
And with thy delicate and lovely form
Wouldst thou shield him from each dark, impending storm.

Arkadelphia, Ar., 1854.

I am giving you this poem to let you see the kind of teachers our people employed and the sympathetic, gentle heart poured out in the song of the stern "Yankee" schoolmaster.

Sister Nannie taught the younger children at home, when the neighborhood school was not in session. This was in accord with the custom of our social rank, but with Sister Kate it was different; she was being "hired" as a teacher, which was a great blow to Pa, who had been very proud of her high mental attainments. But the culture of his children had not been designed by him for a life in the school-room. With most ladies among our associates, accomplishments were for making a good "match" and a good home.

When Sister Mary Helen finished school, she came home

to live. She was beautiful and graceful, and much beloved and admired by the boys and girls of the neighborhood. Her dress was always at the peak of style and she cheerfully suffered the tortures of the instruments of Fashion. But when her health failed later, the doctors said she had lapped her ribs in front in order to have a small waist. Her beaux were numerous, and she spent much of her time visiting her friends in towns of that section of the state and in entertaining them at home.

Sister Nannie was more quiet and thoughtful. In the late fifties one of the neighborhood boys, Calvin Jones, who was in the emigrating party with Sister Nannie, contracted fever and died.[37] They had been from childhood congenial spirits and fast friends. I think at the time of his death he was a law student and that he and Sister Nannie were engaged to be married as soon as he should complete his course. For a long time after this we were uneasy about Sister Nannie's health. She was sent off to the springs and the best medical skill of the section and times were engaged to restore her to her former self. I remember looking through her trunk with her one day and finding a book with Calvin Jones's name written on the fly-leaf. When I asked her about it, tears came into her eyes and she tucked the book away, without answering me. But she never forgot Mother's parting charge, "Take care of my motherless little ones," and it was in the carrying out of this admonition she recovered.

On Sundays she saw that we memorized our hymns and certain selections from the Bible, learned our Sunday School lessons and read good books. During the week, she taught us faithfully in Webster's blue-back speller, MacGuffie's readers, Davie's arithmetic, and Watts on the Mind.[38] The rules in these books she made me memorize perfectly. We studied a grammar, also, but I have forgotten the name of the author, though not the rules.

Pa so often took Brother Kim out of school to go hunting with him he could not learn at home, so he was sent off to a Mr. Wilkerson's School for Boys. And afterwards Pa spared neither time nor money in his attempt to make Brother Kim an educated gentleman, but he was never a scholar, but a hunter.

Learning continued to be difficult for Sue, also. Sister Nannie would have her locked up in a closet or room for missing her spelling. There she had to stay until she learned the lesson or until Pa came. If he found out that she was being punished for missing her spelling, he would send for her, ask her the first three words of the assignment, and if she spelled these correctly, he would let her go.

One afternoon Ma promised to take us down to the creek fishing and we were to have a picnic, too. But Sue could not go; she had missed her spelling and had to sit in the west room until she knew it. Pa was not at home so there was no help for her. It was with a heavy heart that I started off with the party. Under the influence of the great out-of-doors it seemed that Ma began to regret Sue's not sharing this unusual pleasure so she told Lute and me to return to the house and if we saw Sue studying, to tell her she might come with us and learn her lesson later. When we got in sight of the grove we saw a strange sight. She was swinging to the tail of our largest turkey gobbler and whipping him along the narrow path with a switch. In great excitement we delivered Ma's message. How were we to tell Ma the truth and yet take Sue back with us? That was not beyond our maneuvering minds. We told her we would stay there until she could go to the house and at the proper time give us a signal through the open window to come out and "see her studying." Swiftly she disappeared through the open door and there were sounds of flying feet and quite a commotion for several minutes before quiet reigned and she gave us the signal, a low whistle. Entering the room, we found it in apple-pie order and saw Sue staring at the pages of her speller. Again we delivered the message and soon three happy little girls flew down the narrow path and joined the others fishing in the creek. Long afterwards Honey told me her conscience had never been clear about that deceit, for before she went to chase the turkey she had not looked at her book, but had turned all the chairs in the room upside down in the middle of the floor and then had taken all the cover from the bed and spread it over them.

In the summer of 1859 Sister Kate and the other children at school in Tennessee came home on their vacation. This was a great time for us all, but the close of that summer marked an epoch of loneliness in my life, for Honey returned with Sister Kate to go to school in Sommerville. She and I had been inseparable until then, shielding and sympathizing with each other in our little ups and downs as motherless children. Now I was disconsolate, or would have been but for the little Negroes. I stayed with them all I could. Together we roamed the woods and dragged the streams.

One pleasure was dropping chips of wood in the tar barrel which always stood near the tar kiln and throwing them on the streams to make rainbows on the water. Another pleasure was catching redhorses or stone trotters where the water was shallow.[39] We would dig holes near the streams and see who could catch the most minnows. These we would take to Aunt Rose's house to fry. What a feast they made!

4

The doctors said I must not stay in the school room all day and I was sent to Aunt Rose's house to spin a brooch of thread as soon as I could turn a wheel. I wish you could have seen Aunt Rose. You would not have called her pretty, but to me she was beautiful. I liked to steal off right after breakfast and be at her house when the children were brought in for her to take care of while their mothers worked in the fields.

In cold weather she had ready on their arrival a big fire and a needle full of long, coarse, white thread. When a girl came bringing a sleeping child, it was put in a cradle or trundle bed, then the girl turned her back so Aunt Rose could see if her dress were fastened; if not, out would come the needle and the dress was securely sewed together. Sometimes the mothers would button or tack their children's dresses but I have seen Aunt Rose use a yard or two of thread in this way in one morning.

The cradles for the babies were carried to Aunt Rose's early Monday morning and were kept there until Saturday at noon, when they were returned to the homes of the mothers until after Sunday. Two little babies could lie in one cradle and there were seldom more. Often the larger ones brought their breakfasts in a tin bucket, for their mothers let them sleep as much as possible.

Aunt Rose ever kept bread, I know, and she saw that they ate a plenty. She never refused me a piece with the other children and I enjoyed it. Another treat she offered was a skillet of peas. From the sway pole in the wide fireplace hung a large pot containing a quart or more of peas and a piece of meat. Until the Yankees came, I never saw Aunt Rose's "chist clean o' meat," and she surely could cook good peas. When they were done, she poured out a skilletful which she set in the yard, then called "dinner." How we ran to the side of the house for our half mussel shell! I remember mine was high up on the corner, above those of the little Negroes. The shells procured, we ran to the skillet and dipped in our "spoons" until the skillet was empty and had to be refilled. What fun we had! How good the peas tasted! But just let anyone say, "Your Pappy!" and the little Negroes were left alone and I would be found spinning, carding, picking cotton (lint), as the assigned task might be.

Aunt Rose was doctor as well as nurse and kept a medicine chest; turpentine, castor oil, Jerusalem oak or Worm-seed syrup, and sulphur were the contents I remember. She practiced on us, as well as on the colored children, for we took to her our cuts, sores, and other simple ailments. There were certain disease preventives which she administered regularly and we were lined up in two rows, one of white children the other of colored children, for these to be given. Sulphur and molasses came in the spring, two or three times. I afterwards learned that Aunt Rose would hold Honey's nose as she did ours when she came to her, but there was no medicine in the spoon. Honey was her favorite and she hated to give her the mean stuff. I suppose she did not need it. But I was always delicate looking and had to take everything.[40]

I think now I would have been stronger if I had been allowed to eat more solid food at the regular meals. It was considered coarse for a girl to eat heavily; therefore, we had an "allowance" of two biscuits for breakfast, a small piece of bread with meat and vegetables at dinner and a glass of milk with bread at night. This was not enough for me and being unusually active, I filled up on trash between times.

Once I ate too many huckleberries and thinking I was going to die, slipped off down to Aunt Rose's house for help. Her big bed was, to me, always spotless and no child dared touch it. On this occasion I was honored by being laid between her sheets. But she soon saw that I was too sick for her practice and sent me to the house. I crept upstairs to hide, for I knew I would be scolded and perhaps whipped, for eating so greedily. Here, mourning in bed with a high fever, Aunt Helen Levy, who was visiting at home, found me. I remember when she pulled off my stockings, with the big holes tied down in the shoes, she said, "Poor little motherless child." I was tenderly put to bed, a doctor was summoned and it was some time before I was again "on the wind."

I used to have big meetings with the colored children. These were conducted in a corner of the fence around Aunt Rose's house. A plank stuck through cracks about three feet from the ground served as a pulpit and a long plank across the wide part of the corner was for the congregation to sit on. What singing and shouting we had with the preaching, particularly after a protracted meeting in our church.

Once about ten o'clock in the morning, when Becky came from the field to feed her baby and she and Aunt Rose were sitting in front of the door listening to us, I left someone else preaching and slipping in between the colored women, asked them to teach me a new song, sung at the last meeting. When I thought I knew the tune and was returning to teach it to the little Negroes, I heard Aunt Rose say, "She sho gwine to be a good 'oman." "Jest as good as Satan," replied Becky.

Aunt Rose knit Pa gloves—red and black striped, fancy stitch. Pa bought her a red and black dress when he went to New Orleans. The Harrises did not have so many Negroes; when Kate worked in the field her child was cared for by Mrs. Harris.

One of my chief delights was stealing watermelons from Mr. Scott's patch. The whole crowd of Negro children, nurses and babies, would follow me to the fence, where I would tie bark on my feet to hide my tracks and bring out several melons to where my followers stood watching. These we would slip to Aunt Rose's house and then have a great feast, Aunt Rose helping us. I now believe that all the time Mr. Scott knew who got the melons and humored me. I know I never hid my tracks.

Among the most pleasing recollections of my childhood days is that of attending the yearly colored meetings held in old Manchester Church, two and a half miles from home. The same building served as a place of worship for both white and colored of the community. It was near the school house, but of course the colored children were not allowed to go to school.[41]

In the summer, after the cotton and corn had been laid by, Dr. Hunter of the Methodist Church held a meeting of one or two weeks and said the white people must attend, as they did, sitting in their carriages and buggies left at the six open windows, or on the back benches of the church, which were reserved for them. The Strongs, Jones, Harrises, and most of the other families around attended these meetings. The black folks came from eight or ten miles away and at times the church could not hold them.

To me the most conspicuous among the Negroes was a bright colored woman, accompanied by a little bright girl, who attended the services regularly. They wore pretty silk dresses and nice shoes and would drive up on the grounds in a fine buggy drawn by a fat horse which she hitched to a particular tree every day. Then taking the child by the hand, she would walk majestically into the church and down the length of the aisle to her seat on the front bench. She did not seem to know many of the other colored people nor care to get acquainted with them. Aunt Rose said they came from a plantation 'way down the river.

From home the farm wagons carried the dinners, the old colored women, and the little children. The other Negroes walked. A buggy and carriage were for Ma and the other white folks. Pa at times went, but generally kept the house while all the others were away. Sometimes we children were allowed to walk with our black mammy and her husband Uncle John W. He was the hero of my childhood, for he often carried me on his shoulders and told me funny stories. I thought this better than the carriage. If the carriage passed, we would sometimes crawl in but it seems to me it was always filled with visitors and other members of the family.

At the church, one wagon was drawn into the shade where someone from each family saw that the dinner was safe before going to the church. I fear the white people who sat at the windows enjoyed the talk and actions of the colored people more than they did the preaching.

Dr. Hunter was a gifted, magnetic speaker and at times held his audience spellbound, while again he stirred up a tumult. I remember once a woman screamed and jumped up and down while he was describing the beauties of heaven. For a while he stood the interruptions very patiently, then leaning over the pulpit said, "You stop jumping up there like a chicken with its head cut off!" He spoke to the close of his sermon without further interruption. Often when disturbed by the shouting he would sit down in the pulpit until all was quiet.[42]

The mourners' bench was usually crowded and I have never since seen or heard such shouting. Once Uncle Billy's niece Beck was so happy it took two to hold her. One who knew her said, "There will be a fight when Beck gets home." I don't know but what she saw Jenny tear Beck's borrowed dress, but I do know there was a big fight, as predicted, and Beck was the leader.

Uncle Lany Strong was a colored preacher and Uncle Billy was an exhorter. These two often sat in the pulpit with the white preachers and prayed most fervently. I remember Uncle Billy once prayed, "Oh good Lord, wake these sinners. Shake 'um over hell, but don't let 'um fall in."

One protracted meeting was held about the time of a passing of Halley's comet. As Brother Hunter preached, he said that some day it might go whirling through space, strike our earth with its tail, and slap it to atoms. That scared all sleep from my eyes and often at night I would lie awake wondering when the comet with the long tail would come again.[43]

After the close of each big meeting the converts were baptized. Some were sprinkled, but others were immersed in the Ouachita River, for the Methodist Church accepted this form of baptism. However, Pa never allowed his slaves to be baptized by immersion and some of them secretly lamented this. Aunt Rose said folks could not go to Heaven unless they went under the water. There was a question in my childish mind as to which was right, Pa or Aunt Rose, so I read my Bible through for the first time to learn for myself how the Lord meant for me to be baptized. After doing this, I accepted the baptism administered long before by the strange preacher from Little Rock and joined the Methodist Church. I will say here, that when the war was over and our slaves were set free, all of them went down to the river and were immersed.

In the nearby churches protracted meetings were held especially for the white people. Moreover, we had camp meetings, usually at camp grounds located at some health resort. Our house was a home for both the Methodist and the Presbyterian preachers; they would bring their families there for visits of several days or weeks. In summer we kept open house and emigrants and travellers were gladly welcomed. Among our annual summer visitors were Pa's nieces who had moved from North Carolina to Camden.

On one occasion Cousin Martha Bullock was visiting us during a protracted meeting at old Bethlehem Church. Much interest was being shown by all the community. One night as I lay sleeping in the trundle bed in Pa's room I was awakened by a strange noise. After listening for some time I realized that someone was weeping and then footsteps were heard on the stair. Pa sat up in bed as Cousin Martha Bullock entered the room clapping her hands and shouting, "Uncle Charles, I am so happy! I am so happy! I have found my saviour! Sing to me!" Pa seemed happy, too, as well as surprised and embarrassed. Emily and Bell, two of the maids, were sleeping on pallets on the floor near enough to be easily called for service. "Emily, Emily," Pa called, "Go get your daddy to sing for Miss Marthy."

And while Emily and Bell went to get Uncle Billy, Cousin Martha told Pa of her long trouble because of her unbelief and of how the "light had come to her as he prayed that night."

When Uncle Billy came, he led in several farm hands who stood with him [around our beds] while they sang "Tis the Old Ship of Zion," "Walk Easy to de Promised Land," and other Negro songs.[44] Tears of joy ran down Pa's and Cousin Martha's cheeks as they sang. Uncle Billy talked to her and they rejoiced together that she had found her Saviour.

Then she became calm, the members of the choir filed out to their respective homes and Cousin Martha crept back upstairs. With wide open eyes I nestled down under the cover while peace again reigned in the "big" house.

What year it was, I do not remember, but once Pa came home from Arkadelphia and said Mr. Patton wished him to stay in town and entertain the delegates to some meeting of the church courts. Mr. Scott carried Lute to her foster mother, Mrs. Jesse Harris, Uncle Billy took me on a horse to Dr. Tenny's where I had been invited to stay, and one of the older girls looked after the house-keeping while Pa, Ma, and Mattie, the baby, went to town for a week.[45] They took Aunt 'Riah and her daughters to do the cooking and Betsy, Ma's maid, and her husband went along to wait on the folks and to drive the carriage.

Pa entertained the delegates in the building which had been used for the blind asylum, this institution having been moved to Little Rock.[46] Bedding sufficient for the guests and our family still remained in the house but they borrowed crockery from a store in town. I remember this because one of the plates and one of the preserves stands got broken and Pa bought and brought them home after the meeting. The stands were beautiful and had only a nicked place in one of the tops. In those days we had no ice in summer and a one-horse wagon went from home every day with chickens and fresh vegetables.

Aunt 'Riah had always bossed her kitchen and was called

the best cook in the state. Ma said she looked out of her window one morning and saw a fire in the yard large enough to roast an ox. The cook there wanted her way and Aunt 'Riah wanted hers. Saying "Take de kitchen, an' have yer way," Aunt 'Riah had left the kitchen, kindled the fire in the yard and prepared breakfast in the yard.

There was no one at Dr. Tenny's where I was staying except Mrs. Tenny and their cook. I had a lonely time until the cook's husband came on Friday night. Then I had a nice time for he taught me to whistle like a jaybird and a mockingbird and he told me lots of tales. I surely enjoyed having someone to talk to; I never went to the church.

In fact, I think I never attended the Presbyterian Church but once before the war. Then two of the old ladies wore long sun-bonnets and pretty plaid shawls. Governor Flanagan's wife invited us home with them to dinner.[47] On our way home I said to Sister Mary Helen, "Mrs. Flanagan has silver forks with four prongs." (I had seen only steel forks with two or three prongs.) Sister Mary Helen replied, "The forks are brass; much of the plating is worn off."

This reminds me that once I went with Sister Mary Helen to a neighbor's to spend the night. There was a crowd of young people there and while they were in the midst of their fun and frolic, the head of the home said in a firm, reverent tone, "Let's go to prar." Instantly we all knelt and he led in earnest, fervent prayer. We had always quietly taken seats in a circle while Pa read the Bible before leading us in prayer. After we had risen from our seats, I crept up to Sister Mary Helen and confided in whispered tones, "Don't they have funny prayers here?" Afterwards I learned that I had been overheard and the old man never had family prayers again. It surely hurt me.

Honey was as much of a rambler and "tom-boy" as I. We

had spent a great part of a summer roaming over our old haunts and attempting new projects. One afternoon that fall we called our two rabbit dogs, Lad and Gam, and went out hunting. The north persimmon tree was at least a mile away but we struck out for it while the dogs hunted the woods. We had scarcely reached the tree when barks from the dogs let us know we had found game. Off we ran in their direction, now following a pig-path, now jumping over the brambles and then through the briar patch and on across a little branch. Here we saw what made us glad! Gam was sitting before a hollow in a large tree and across the branch Lad was scratching at the hollow in another tree. Out came Honey's bowie knife and a twister was soon made from a small bush.[48] With this she tried in vain to pull down Mr. Hare. Then we cut some pine splinters from the heart of a rotten pine log and started a fire in the mouth of the hollow. On this we piled leaves which caused such a smoke that the rabbit fell and was grabbed.

We took him across the creek, where a twister was soon caught in the hide of the hare in the other hollow. When Honey, who held the captured rabbit, saw me struggling to twist the other one out, she laid hers on the ground and he bounded for freedom, but the watchful dogs caught him before he got far.

While working at my rabbit, we heard a roar in the first tree and on looking up, it seemed that the flames from the top of it nearly reached the sky. Honey sprang back across the branch, threw some wet leaves on the fire, then great handfuls of mud, which caused such a steam the flames up the hollow were extinguished and soon every spark of the fire was out. Boasting that we were rivals of Diana, we reached home with our game. Aunt 'Riah and Betsy were told of our scare, but I guess the grown folks (white) never knew about it until we were grown.

Hog killing time was a great event on the plantation. On the day before great loads of wood and several of rock were hauled to the slaughter pen, out some distance behind the Negro cabins. At four o'clock in the morning the horn, a large pink lined conc shell about the size of a calf's head, was blown by Mr. Scott and all the Negro men rolled out of bed to set fire to the previously laid heaps and to fill the vats with water from a nearby branch. These vats were made of two pine logs about six feet long, with the side of each one sawed off. These were put in frames and wedged together, the seams having been chinked with cotton. Rocks were put in the fire of pine knots and when red hot were thrown into the vats, thus heating the water for scalding.

By the time we children had dressed and stolen out the back way to the scene of action, the fires were beautiful in the gloaming, with their flames of yellow, red, and purple dancing in the chilly morning breeze.

Amid songs and mirth, the work of removing the hair from the slain hogs was begun and soon they were hanging in rows on long elevated poles.

We were given pig tails to roast in the fire, but as we prepared this tempting morsel, one eye was ever on the look-out for Pa, while we attempted in every way to please Mr. Scott, who seldom denied the three little motherless girls anything. Now and then a Negro woman would come begging a piece of liver to cook for breakfast, or a maw to cook for dinner.

One morning I was near one end of the fire broiling a piece of liver when a Negro boy passed and said, "Yer pappy." Liver and fire were left behind as, bent low, I ran past the row of cabins, behind the shrubbery of the grave-yard, down the lane leading to the back gate, then into the house. I slipped cautiously into the west room and lay on the lounge.

In a short time Lute, who had been with me, came in and sat in disgrace in Ma's room. Soon I walked in, rubbing my eyes, to be anxiously asked, "Where have you been?" "On the lounge in the west room," I replied, but I felt guilty of gross deceit when I heard Ma say to Pa, "Harriet was asleep in the west room."

The first year of the war Pa killed sixty hogs. A big molasses barrel filled with lard was set in an opening made in the floor of the lumber-room. This is how we kept the lard cool enough not to melt in warm weather. Before the war Pa bought pickled pork in New Orleans for the slaves. Even during the war meat, meal, and flour were seldom scarce at home; neither were corncobs which, during the war, we burnt and used the ashes to make soda water for our bread.

After the Yankees had captured the ports of the Mississippi and Pa could not go on his annual journey to New Orleans for supplies, we sorely felt the need of things we could not raise on the farm.

One night after my supper of bread and milk, I lay awake in my trundle bed and was listening to snatches of conversation which floated out from the dining room as the older members of the family gathered for their evening meal.

Pa came in from a hunt, tired, sick, and out of sorts. His coffee of ground parched wheat, settled with parched sweet potatoes, was not to his taste; it should have been a clear, pretty drink. Storming angrily, he took down his horse whip and struck Aunt 'Riah across her shoulders. Out of my bed I shot, and clad in my night-gown and cap, I rushed into the dining-room, caught Pa's hand and screamed, "You shan't whip Aunt 'Riah! You shan't whip Aunt 'Riah!"

Surprised by my sudden interference, and abashed at his loss of temper, Pa looked at me in helpless amazement and exclaimed, "What must I do with her? What must I do with her?"

Aunt 'Riah, with bowed head shielded by her arm, hastened from the room, weeping more from humiliation than from pain of body, I know, however hard the blow may have been. She had never been struck before, as we knew of, and I never heard of her being punished after. I know Pa was ashamed of himself, for he was tender-hearted as well as high-tempered.

Aunt Patsy said snakes were serpents in Bible times and she was a smart old woman, I knew. She said that after the Serpent gave Eve the apple, God took and turned his legs down and slipped a tight skin on him so he would not move and he had to crawl "on yer stomach befo' yer pappy" the rest of his days. He had some black and speckled children and they all crawled, though they had legs under their skin.

That was a big tale to swallow. With several of the "gang" who were big enough to look for snakes where the high water left drifts of trash, I set out to prove that snakes have legs. We saw several sleeping moccasins on the drift piles. After much work, with long poles we got two or three of them out. These we killed and carried on sticks to the front of Aunt Rose's house, where we built a funeral pile, around which we joined hands and sang:

> God delivered Daniel, and why not ev'yman?
> When man wuz fust created, so godly he appear'd
> But 'cause he et de apple, he wuz sent to death and hell.

As we danced around the funeral pile, the dead snakes squirmed and soon through their skins we thought we saw four legs burst out—two just below the neck and two near the tail. Sister Nannie said they were muscles, but to us they were legs. Aunt Patsy said so, and Aunt Patsy knew about snakes.

One day a box of tulip bulbs came from Grandma Shapherd's in Tennessee. These were highly prized and soon the servants were at work manuring, spading and raking plots on each side of the front porch, where the bulbs were duly planted.

In time broad leaves appeared above ground and in each bunch one or two buds. They grew rapidly, early showing petals of many colors like flowers we had never seen. Neighbors were shown these new wonders and all admired them. However, I thought they would be far more beautiful if the petals did not bend together at the top, concealing their greater brilliancy.

While the grown folks were napping one afternoon, I slipped out and began work on the tulips; each petal was turned back so as to remain open and thus show the glistening colors of different shades of red, yellow, and purple. I was proud of what I had done and when I heard an older sister coming down the stairs I ran to let her know that the tulips had spread at last. She came out and stood aghast at the sight before her. Her fine rare flowers looked ruined. When she could speak she said "Tulip petals stand up, as they were. Now go and turn every one back."

To work I went and after much labor had them all in place as before. This time I did not get my usual scolding but I was very disappointed to know that tulips hid their greatest beauty.

In Aunt Rachel's yard was a nice seedling apple tree which bore sweet apples in season. On our plantation apple trees were rare. At this particular time no one was in sight and I concluded to climb to the branches and sample the ripening fruit.

As I bit the first apple, Aunt Rachel turned the corner of the house, "Never mind," she screamed, "I am sho gwine ter tell Miss Mary an' yer pappy is gwine ter whip yer."

Quickly I slid down the tree; I knew Aunt Rachel liked to make quilts, so I said, "If you don't tell on me, I'll give you lots of nice bed-quilt pieces."

We made the bargain and she gave me several apples. I was afraid to ask for the scraps, but when Ma was out calling and the coast was clear, I got her scrap bag, selected a good roll, regardless of value or color, and paid my debt.

One fall Pa had gotten several bushels of apples from somewhere and we had them spread on the floor of the smoke house. On this particular morning there was no uncertain odor in the air, not the perfume of our delicious fruit, either. The dogs were barking around the smoke house so several of the household gathered out in the yard, suspecting that a polecat must be hidden about the building. Some people call polecats skunks.

To settle the matter, Pa sent for the smokehouse key, turned the bolt, and pushed open wide the door. The object of interest rushed past Pa and as she did so sprinkled him from head to foot by a flash of her bushy tail. He turned, with his usual expression of disgust, "Er shucks," and walked into the house to change his clothes while the dogs chased the frightened animal down the bottoms.

"Thar are young'uns under thar," said one of the old darkies, pointing to the smoke house. "Dat old mammy cat got in de house through dat hole back o' de 'lasses barrel."

"Under thar" I went, returning soon with a couple of white and black spotted polecat kittens held carefully in my apron. How proud I was! They were the most beautiful things I had ever seen.

The family was horrified and my treasures were ordered to be killed instantly. I was rushed to my room, where my tears fell, and that not in silence, while I was scrubbed and my clothes changed. The garments I took off were buried with Pa's to destroy the odor.

Many of our apples were ruined and some of the family teased me about trying to raise polecats, but I never got over the loss of my treasures and the cruel treatment to the beautiful, innocent looking baby skunks.

When I was a child I attempted almost everything I saw anyone else do. I even tried to plow once, to my great sorrow. As I have told you, Damon and Shadrack were two great favorites on the plantation. They were kind to us children so all of us loved them. Often we would save our biscuits for them. Corn bread was more plentiful than flour. One day I went out to where Shadrack was bedding some corn rows and asked him to let me run a row. He never refused me anything so handed me the plow handles. I managed to make a row or two, as crooked as a snake, but I thought I had done fine.

That night Dr. Hunter came. As he looked over the field with Mr. Scott, our overseer, he said, "Scott, I always thought you had the straightest corn rows in the country and am astonished to see such crooked ones in front here."

I heard this, thought of my work, and felt guilty but said nothing and the subject of plowing was dropped. Some time afterwards I told Aunt 'Riah that Mr. Hunter was to hold the big meeting for the colored folks, thinking she would be pleased.

"I don' want ter hear none er his talk," she replied. "He dun come over here medlin wid our work an' had Shadrack whooped. Mr. Anderson is de onliest white preacher dat has got any 'ligion and dat keers fer us."

Most of the black folks felt as she did and I understood that my plowing and Mr. Hunter's thoughtless remark about it had caused him to lose influence among them.

However, he held the meeting and I think they got over the bitter feeling. In later years when the politicians were looking for a man they thought both white and black would unite in electing governor of Arkansas, Dr. Hunter was their choice. But his wife told him the offer was the temptation of the devil, who was trying to get him to stop serving the Lord to "serve tables." So he never ran for governor but became president of a Methodist college.

June and Damon were missing! Mystery shrouded the plantation. The other Negroes seemed to know nothing of their whereabouts and Pa and Mr. Scott could learn nothing about them from the neighbors. There was no favorable reply to their advertisements for runaway slaves and it was as though the earth had opened and swallowed the Negroes.

But late one evening in the early fall, as Pa walked up and down the front porch with his hands clasped behind him, he stopped and looked long and thoughtfully out towards the river. Then calling Brother Kim, he told him to go over to Mr. Jones's and ask him to come early the next morning to go hunting with him.

Pa ordered his breakfast by light and soon afterwards Mr. Jones joined Pa and Brother Kim at the front gate. When it was suggested that some of the Negroes should go to drive the deer past the stands, Pa said they would not be needed for they would "still" hunt. This meant that the hunters would stand and watch for the deer to come to the salt licks.

When the three had gotten some distance from the house, Pa told Mr. Jones and Brother Kim about seeing smoke rising from over the cane brake, the evening before, and added that he believed June and Damon were hidden in the brake.

Brother Kim said they rode as quietly as they could that the slaves might not hear the horses and every now and then they would get down and look for tracks in the soft mud. After traveling this way for several miles, they discovered a very narrow but well worn path leading from our plantation into the brake, thus showing that there had been constant communication between the runaways and some of our slaves.

Tying their horses, they cautiously followed this trail until they came to the river. Here at first they could find no signs of a crossing but farther down the stream they saw near the bank a large stone and then another and another, so by long leaps one could cross the river on these stones. Reaching the opposite bank, they found a continuation of the trail, which led out into a small open space farther down the river and some distance from it. There in a kind of cave which they had dug lay the two Negroes, fast asleep. Having foraged for food all night, they were completely exhausted and off their guard.

As the three white men, with guns and ropes in hand, stood over them, Pa called "You, June, get up from there!" Like they had been shot, the two Negroes jumped up, half dazed. They were easily tied and were soon trotting down the path in front of their captors, going home.

They were both punished but Damon's punishment was not so severe as his companion's for June had always given trouble, while Damon was somewhat of a favorite. Some time after this June made another attempt to run away alone and was drowned in the river.

After June's death, Damon told us he wanted to come back when he found out that June was running away but he was afraid June would kill him, as he threatened. When his good conduct had restored him to his former position on the plantation, he said one day to Pa, "Marster, one mornin' when yer was out huntin' fer us, yer sot for hours on a big ol' log at de edge er de bottom an' I wuz right behin' yer, covered up in the leaves. It seemed ter me lack yer sot dar forever. I wuz so stiff I could hardly move when you had gone away."

I was a Bullock and raised to work, though I was small and delicate. Too delicate for a whole day in the schoolroom, I was sent to Aunt Rose's house to perform some active tasks. We were warned never to go between Uncle Billy and the gin when they were ginning cotton. One afternoon I had something to tell Uncle Billy so I stole away from the others and went to the gin house where I climbed the rickety stair and without thinking, ran toward him. But something grabbed my skirt with annoying force; then above the noise of the machinery, Uncle Billy's voice rang out louder than I had ever heard before: "STOP! STOP DAT GIN!"

Things stopped and a small black head was poked in at the door and a wavering voice inquired, "What is it, Daddy?" "Go back ter dem mules," stormed Uncle Billy. He was trembling from head to foot. "Lord Jesus Marster," the old man prayed, as he cleared the gin saw of my thick skirt that held me fast. "Help! Help! Help!"

My dress was of calico, made with rotten thread, so most of the skirt was ripped from the waist, a part of the front was sawed to pulp. With Uncle Billy's help, I gathered the top of my skirt together, and holding it around my waist, I ran around the cotton bale shed, through the horse lot, back of the stable, into dear Aunt Rose's house and arms. In those days skirts were made of three widths of cloth. Only the front of one width was torn. Aunt Rose got her needle and thread, removed the torn part, and had my dress nearly ready to put on when in ran a little darky saying, "Marster is comin'."

Over my head went the dress and when Pa passed the door,

I was carding diligently and singing as loudly as I could, "Whar de Keys ter de Promised Lan'?" "That is right, Harriet, card your rolls,"[49] smilingly said Pa as he passed.

Aunt Rose said I was as white as a sheet. I had mercifully escaped the gin and Pa, but how escape the other white folks? Aunt Rose never told on us but how should I account for the condition of my dress? I watched for an opportunity, slipped up to the house, and stealthily changed my dress, hiding the torn one. It was new, though made of rotten calico. My help was Betsy, Ma's maid. We children and the "gang" said Ma was always ready to show Betsy a kindness and I knew her weakness.

"Ma," I said, walking indifferently into her room, "do you care if I give Betsy that rotten calico dress to put in her quilt?" "Surely not, if you wish," she replied. The waters ran smooth again and no grown white person, as far as I know, heard of my gin scrape until I had passed the whipping line.

Sister Nannie had taught me faithfully until I was ten years old. Then, with a McGuffy's Reader, a Child's geography, and Webster's speller, I started with Brother Kim and Lute to Manchester school, where Dr. Steel was the teacher. The rough walk of two and a half miles was rather long for eight year old Lute. We had to cross Mill Creek and Easley Creek on logs. Our shoes were of stout leather and we had never heard of over-shoes.

The school house was of logs, with a stick chimney and a spacious fireplace. A log was sawed out of the side of the house for a window and a wide plank was hung on leather hinges above the opening for a shutter. This plank was raised to give light on the writing desk in front of the opening. A long bench was placed in front of the writing desk and on the opposite side of the house were two other benches like the ones in the nearby church. Two other benches about eight feet long sat in front of these and the teacher's habitual seat was a chair leaning against one of the two upright boards which supported the mantle piece.

We were late the first morning. Around the room sat Virgie Tinny; John Duke; Kim, Elihu, and Mary Jones; Zan and Willie Littlejohn; George and Robert Gilmer; Zeb and Lafayette Cleveland; and we three Bullocks—Kim, Lute and Hariett—sixteen in all. Soon Pony Phillips walked in, a long, slim boy, who to us girls, seemed six feet of rudeness and meanness.

Pony entered the Civil War in '61 and was soon killed and to tell the truth, we little girls felt that the world was a more pleasant place to live in.[50] Zan and Willie Littlejohn had such red heads that Lute asked who were the red-capped boys.

Lute was still a beautiful child, blue-eyed, rosy-cheeked, brown-haired and quite a pet with all of us. At the opening of the school each morning we read the Bible, each child in turn reading a verse. Once Lute started her verse, "A sower went forth to sow his seed" giving the short sound to the o's. Dr. Steel told her to read it again and the whole school, except us, laughed aloud. Again she read the passage as before. "Call the word right," in anger he commanded the little child. As she hesitated he sent for a switch. Someone whispered "sow", giving the word the correct pronunciation, so she finished her verse and the chapter was completed by the school.

At play-time I ran near Dr. Steel and he caught me. Still burning with indignation because of Lute's recent experience, I scraped my nails across his hand, taking out three pieces of skin and leaving three streaks of bloody flesh. "You wild-cat," he said, and pushed me from him. I was scared and thought I was disgraced but he didn't whip me, as I feared he would.

We carried our dinner to school in a wide-mouthed tin bucket, the top of which fitted snugly, and if food were put into the bucket while hot it tasted tinny. We generally carried a large quinine bottle full of molasses, and biscuits and meat of some sort. We would punch a hole in the side of a biscuit with a finger and fill the hole with molasses. When all the molasses had been eaten in this way, we would fill the bottle with water and drink "switchel water." We always had plenty of butter for our lunches, too.

Dr. Steel boarded among the scholars and came to us in the month of December. On the eighteenth of the month that year, I had my first birthday cake and my first sugar candy. Ma said Sister Mary Helen fixed it for the teacher, and maybe she did, for I never had another.

Mr. Steel was a good teacher but he had a bad lot of boys and at least one spit-fire girl in me.

We often rode to school in a spring wagon. Once the boys said they had to go to Cassamassa for school books. They left at noon and stayed until time for school to close and thought it a good joke. Another time, while Dr. Steel slept at recess, the boys told us to hide under the church benches and they took old Queen, the horse, off and hid her. When Dr. Steel awoke, not a child was in sight but when he called us to school the second time, I came out of hiding and told on the others. They called me a sneak and the boys, coming in when the afternoon session was half over, gave me a good scolding.

The Civil War began the next year, Dr. Steel left, and we went back to studying under Sister Nannie.

Harriet Bailey Bullock before her marriage to Nathaniel B. Daniel.
Courtesy of Clara McCaskill.

Harriet Bailey Bullock Daniel and her daughter, Sara.

Nathaniel Beverly Daniel and Harriet Bailey Bullock Daniel.
Courtesy of Bailey Webb.

Harriet Bailey Bullock Daniel when she was about eighty years old.
Courtesy of Bailey Webb.

Nancy Bullock (Sister Nannie).
Courtesy of Clara McCaskill.

Sara Catherine Bullock Taylor (Sister Kate).
Courtesy of Clara McCaskill.

Thomas Dickinson and Fanny Lynne Bullock Dickinson (Sister Fanny).
Courtesy of Clara McCaskill.

Susan Yancey Bullock (Sue or "Honey").
Courtesy of Clara McCaskill.

Charles Lewis Bullock.
Courtesy of First Presbyterian Church of Arkadelphia.

Martha Linda Bullock McCaskill (Mattie).
Courtesy of Clara McCaskill.

Cornelia Fletcher Bullock Williams (Nell).
Courtesy of Clara McCaskill.

Sylvan Home before 1940s renovation.
Courtesy of Clara McCaskill.

Sylvan Home during renovation. Notice size of logs.
Courtesy of Clara McCaskill.

Sylvan Home after renovation.
Courtesy of Claude McCaskill.

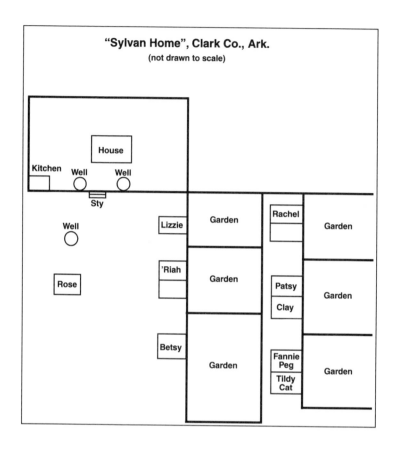

Figure 1. Site Plan of Sylvan Home drawn by Bailey Daniel.

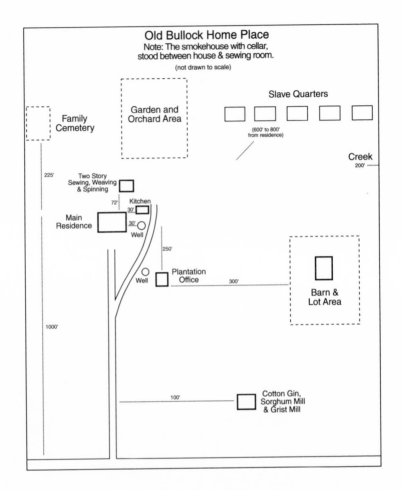

Figure 2. Site Plan of Sylvan Home drawn by Neill McCaskill in 1992.

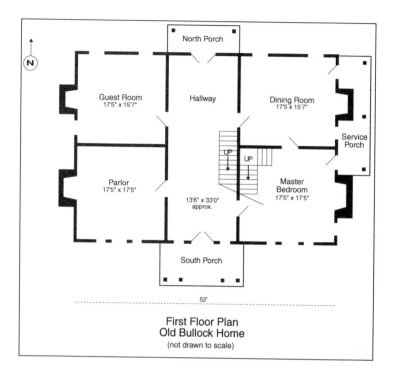

N

North Porch

| Guest Room | Hallway | Dining Room |
| 17'5" x 15'7" | | 17'5 x 15'7" |

Service Porch

UP UP

Parlor		Master
17'5" x 17'5"		Bedroom
		17'5" x 17'5"

13'6" x 33'0"
approx.

South Porch

52'

First Floor Plan
Old Bullock Home
(not drawn to scale)

Figure 3. Plan of first floor of Sylvan Home
drawn by Neill McCaskill in 1982.

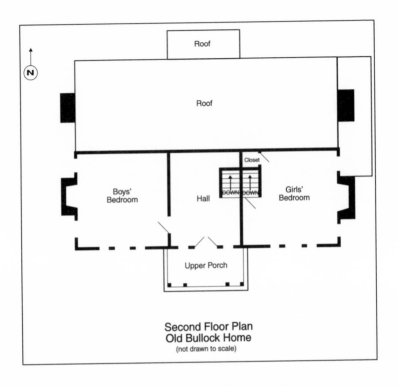

Figure 4. Plan of second floor of Sylvan Home
drawn by Neill McCaskill in 1992.

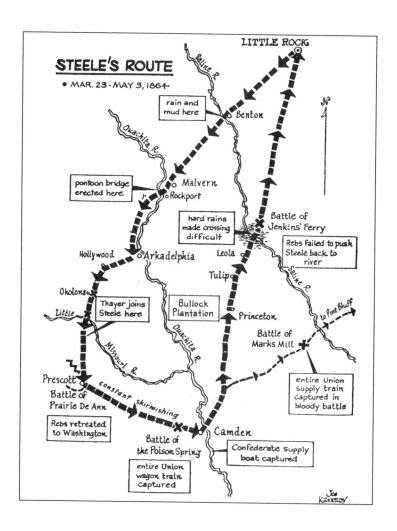

Figure 5. *Map showing Bullock plantation in relation to battles in the Camden Expedition of General Frederick Steele.* Courtesy of Dr. John Ferguson.

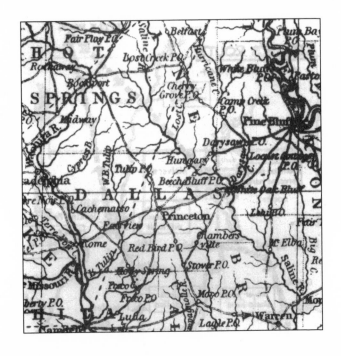

Figure 6. Map of Dallas County, Arkansas, in 1856.
Courtesy of Special Collections Division,
University of Arkansas Libraries, Fayetteville.

*Location of Dallas
and Clark counties.*

5

It seemed to me that Mr. Jones and Mr. Littlejohn came over home just to quarrel with Pa and at times I thought Mr. Littlejohn would strike him with his uplifted cane. I wondered what it was all about—state rights, secession, slaves and the Union, of which they were talking so excitedly. I remember Pa would say, time and again, in very emphatic tones, "If the South wants states rights, she must raise the United States flag and fight under the stars and stripes, then every Democrat in the North will help us, but they will never leave the Union and I cannot blame them."

I was only eleven years old, but I understood that there was something terrible the matter, and it was about my friends, the colored people. One morning Pa came to the breakfast table, drank a cup of coffee, then turned with his face to the back of his chair and bowed his head in prayer. We had just had family prayers, too. That day he fasted and prayed for the Union. It was the only time I ever knew him to fast.

They said if there should be a war, Brother Tom would have to go and fight. How I trembled when I thought of this! He had finished school in Somerville, Tennessee, and was clerking in Pa's drug store in Arkadelphia. He often came home and was my hero for he always took my part when Brother Kim and I had a quarrel. The latter was just a few years my senior and we differed seriously, even to blows. I thought Brother Tom was as handsome as a picture, too, and I remember how indignant I was when I heard a girl say someone was ugly as little old Tom Bullock.

Although Pa thought holding to the Union was the only way to keep the slaves, he was ever a staunch Southerner. Yet some of the people in our part of the state thought he should be sent North or be killed, fearing that he would act as a traitor to the Southern cause. One man in the neighborhood, who held views like Pa's, was found by his wife one morning hanging dead from a tree in front of his house.

Once Pa's own cousin, Judge Sommerville, had soldiers sent to take him prisoner.[51] Pa saw the soldiers coming, met them at the gate saying, "Come in, gentlemen. Supper will soon be ready. Come in and tell us the latest news of the war." Entirely ignorant of their mission, he entertained them most hospitably, expressing in every way his thorough sympathy with the South. After some time the soldiers returned to Tulip without the intended captive and told the authority which had sent them, if all the citizens of the country were as loyal as Colonel Bullock the South was safe. It was long after that we found out the true object of the soldiers' visit had been to do away with Pa as they had his more unfortunate neighbor.

Early in 1861 Sister Kate came home from Tennessee, bringing Sister Anna Booker and Honey with her. I was glad to see my older sisters, but my joy at seeing Honey again knew no bounds. She had grown much taller, and I thought wiser, but as of old was my constant champion and defender. I was always so heedless and outspoken, always getting into so much trouble I needed someone to love me through it all and make allowances for me. Honey did this as long as she lived.

Sister Kate had not been home long ere the house was all astir with preparations for her wedding. She and a distant relative, Cousin Sam Taylor, a wealthy planter who lived near Sommerville, were married and soon after the wedding they returned to their Tennessee home.

In the spring news reached us that there had been fighting in Virginia. Brother Tom, with the other men in the neighborhood who had volunteered, joined Captain Gray's company under Colonel Alexander. I remember the neighbors gave a fish-fry in honor of the departing soldiers. It seemed to me the whole country was turned out to see them march. The soldiers wore white uniforms with blue trimmings and to us everything looked grand. Many said the war would soon be over, but Pa gravely shook his head. In a few days the soldiers left for the east to join General Lee.[52]

Soon after Brother Tom left for the East, soldiers came in crowds from Texas and camped for several days near us. They made hair ropes with which to hobble their horses and they had never seen peaches nor strawberries before. There were many cases of measles in this camp and several soldiers came to our house to be cared for, as we were the only people in the neighborhood who had had measles.

And many people passed home, going to Texas to save their slaves. Sometimes they would rest several days with us. Passing scouts stopped once a week. We heard that at Benton they usually met ladies who brought them news from the Northern army. We were always glad to see these scouts. Ma would get them to bring needles, pins, and other small useful articles to us on return. Once she sent for wool and cotton cards. The scout amused us by saying he had to buy a pair of broken cards, and pay full price for them, as he could get no others. Cards were considered better if "broken" by use. Before Sister Nannie would let us use the toothbrushes she bought from them, she always boiled them thoroughly. One scout told her that birch limbs made the best toothbrushes, but she smilingly replied that she preferred the hair ones. I suppose he meant the little sticks were to be chewed at one end, thus forming a small brush for the teeth. At first scouts slept in the house; later they went to the bottoms for the night.

Though we always entertained hospitably, often sending out to the road to invite travelers in, these travelers meant much more than the ordinary work for the slaves and some of the visitors were not always easy to serve. Aunt 'Riah said one old man was always fussing about everything and she despised to do anything for him. Once he asked her to bring him a tub of warm water for his feet. She brought it rather hot and when he asked her to see if it were cool enough she ran her hand down by the side of the tub with the tough palm out and held it in the water, as though it were quite the right temperature. After satisfying him, she hastened from the room as he soused both feet in the tub, only to leap out with a cry of surprised pain. Of course, he was not seriously hurt and Aunt 'Riah had a good chuckle, but not where the white folks would see.

One morning Billy Mills, one of the soldiers who had stayed at home to be nursed through his spell of measles, rode up and was hailed by us all with delight. We had become fond of him; besides, we were eager to hear the news. After dinner the whole family followed Billy to the porch to hear him continue to relate his own experiences and tell what he knew about the armies. Even Ma, who had been confined to her room for some time with illness, ventured out among the eager listeners on the front porch.

As we listened, we looked up the road and saw two men riding rapidly towards the house. Ma started in, but faced two armed soldiers standing at the back hall door. Turning into her room she saw a soldier at each window. On through the dining room she rushed, heedless of the guards and did not stop until she was out in the yard, where flinging herself into Betsy's arms, she cried, "O save me, Betsy! Save me and my children!"

She was so frightened she did not recognize Pa and Mr. Duke, who were following her, but continued to them her plea of mercy, "Please! Please! Do not kill us," she begged again and again.

At length she recognized Pa and then Mr. Duke, a much beloved neighbor.[53] The Southern soldiers, knowing how nervous Ma was, had gotten Mr. Duke to come with them to the house to capture Billy. They said Billy had killed and robbed a scout and was returning to Texas with the money. He went off quietly with the soldiers. One rumor said he had thrown the money in the river, so they could never prove the deed on him; another said he divided it with the men who turned him loose. Either way we children were glad our friend Billy was set free.

About this time news came that Brother Tom had been wounded in battle. There was nothing for us to do but to wait in anxious grief for what might be, and to pray. For days we lived expecting some kind of news. At last there came a cheerful letter from him saying he was being cared for in the home of a good old Presbyterian Elder near Milton, North Carolina, and hoped to soon be well enough to visit relatives farther east in Granville, until he should be able to return to the army.

When Brother Tom returned home after the war, he told us of his many interesting experiences, especially of his visits among his relatives. He said he spent much time at Aunt Nancy's (Charles Bullock's sister) and she had several sons in the war. One, Nat Daniel, was about his age and he had invited him to come out west when the war was over.

When the Yankees passed Memphis Governor Flanagan borrowed Pa's carriage and horses to move his family from Little Rock to Texas. He went to live in Washington, Arkansas, to which place the capital of Arkansas was temporarily moved. With Pa's permission, he carried the horses on to Texas, where he kept them until after the war.

As the Northern army advanced up the Mississippi River, the Confederate government ordered all the cotton on hand to be burned, but our soldiers, thinking this was wrong, warned the planters of their own approach to execute the order. The farmers had been ordered not to plant cotton, but to plant wheat, corn, and other food stuff. Pa, however, planted some cotton each year and stored it under the shed. Of course, there was no market for it.

In the first year of the war, Mr. Scott planted the largest crop of cotton we had ever had. The hands called the fields the white oceans. I think we made one hundred and one bales that year. When the order for the destruction of the cotton reached us, Pa moved much of it from the shed to the lumber room, the meat house, the kitchen loft, and many bales were taken to the woods and hidden. When the soldiers came to destroy it, they looked only in the shed and did not even open the lint room door. Therefore, when the war closed, we had over two hundred bales of cotton and I think Pa got thirty cents a pound for it when it was sold.[54]

Peace or war, Pa wished the younger children to be educated and he was most fortunate in procuring the services of Miss Mary Cooper of Staunton, Virginia. Until the outbreak of the war she had taught in the family of Governor Roan but now she was staying in the family of a music teacher, Mr. Barcus of Tulip, whose boarding school had closed.[55] As she could not get back home on account of the war, she said she would be glad to live in a reliable family and teach for food and raiment, if she could be compensated after the war, provided her employer should then be able. It was well that in these trying times the whole responsibility of our education did not rest on Sister Nannie. Mr. Barcus had six pianos and he let us have what he said was the best one. Miss Mary Cooper gave us music lessons.

Soon after Miss Mary came to live with us, our shoe maker made her a pair of nice shoes from the leather of some buggy cushions. Some of our old silk dresses were scraped to lint, mixed with cotton, and woven into dresses for her. Palmetto was bleached and plaited for her a hat like ours. Therefore, she was nicely and comfortably dressed without much cost. We sang with feeling:

> My homespun dress is plain, I know
> My hat is palmetto too:
> But that just shows what Southern girls
> For Southern rights will do.

During the war four wheels and two looms ran most of the time, weaving cloth for our large family and for the numerous slaves. It was Macklin's business to keep the plantation well shod. He cut, sawed, and fashioned his "pigs," or lasts, from maple, and his shoe wax was of wax from the pine. Usually the leather was made from hides tanned in large vats in the tan-yard.

We used the roots of ever-green ivy for red dye; maple and sweet-gum for purple; and red and white-oak bark for black dyes. Madder dyed woolens a purplish pink. Hickory bark dyed yellow. Used alum to set the dye; soaked materials in copperas water before dying brown or black with walnut hulls or red-oak bark. Sweet-gum dyed a pretty drab, if set with copperas. Cedar dyed drab, but not a pretty shade. Plum root dyed a pretty brown. Poke berries dyed a nice magenta, but would fade.

Hoop skirts were in fashion at that time and we made the stays for these from oak splits, scraped very thin. Once Brother Kim caught some coons and sent the skins off and had them made into a hat which was so nice looking even Pa enjoyed wearing it. This might have been before the war, I cannot remember.

Miss Mary Cooper had red hair and her exceedingly rough complexion was full of pimples. When she chalked (you call it powdered) her face, we children would say secretly she had set up her snow capped mountains. However, she was a splendid teacher, with a lovable disposition, and a great blessing in our home. I corresponded with her as long as she lived and through the years her cheerful letters brightened many a lonely hour.

In April of 1863 there was another wedding at home. Sister Anna Booker married a handsome, wealthy young doctor, Horace Palmer, from an aristocratic family in Sommerville, Tennessee, she met at school. He was a good doctor. She was only nineteen, and my mother had said she hoped all her daughters would wait until they reached the age of twenty-one before getting married and Pa had agreed with her in this. But now, he heartily approved of this marriage, for Sister Anna was a rather lively young girl and he was glad to see her settled in life with so promising a son-in-law. There was cleaning and cooking and the extra commotion that always attended these affairs, even in war times.

After the marriage, Sister Anna and her husband stayed on at home for he was to go east and join the Southern army. One afternoon the bride and groom went out for a drive. When they reached the far gate at the head of the avenue, on their return, the boy was not there to open it, as was the custom, so Dr. Palmer jumped out of the carriage and threw the reins over the spatter board, instead of giving them to Sister Anna. The horses became frightened, sprang through the gate, and rushed down the avenue, hurling the carriage from side to side of the road. Without the reins Sister Anna was helpless and was thrown out on the side of the road when the horses made the first spring. Fortunately she landed on a soft spot and was only lightly bruised; but the new carriage was completely wrecked, and was never used again as a vehicle. The leather of the upholstery was made into shoes by Macklin. I have worn several pair of them. And I suppose the other parts of the vehicle met other war-time needs.

Bro. Kim often went hunting with the colored boys and we longed to join them, but were told that little girls must stay at home many times when little boys could go. Dr. Palmer never hunted, even by day, much to Pa's disgust. Once when we were teasing Pa to let us go with the boys, we got him to say we might if Dr. Palmer would go with us. The latter was not present. Off we went and won from him the promise to go if Pa said we might. That was all we wanted. Brother Kim was told that Pa had said we might go hunting and Dr. Palmer had promised to go with us.

That night was as good as any for the trapped doctor to keep his promise. Brother Kim, with three colored boys carrying pine for the torch lights and Uncle Josh Strong's old possum dogs, Gam and Lad, called us from the back gate as he started. With our maids Belle and Ida we set out in high spirits thinking surely we could catch several possums. Dr. Palmer reluctantly brought up the rear.

Whooping and calling the dogs, we crossed the branch and entered the woods. We girls had often hunted rabbits in the daytime and could follow Brother Kim across streams and through the brambles, even at night. Dr. Palmer said we were half Indian, and much to our disgust, we had to stop now and then to wait for him.

Thus we went nearly to the Negro grave yard, but the dogs found nothing. I know now the boys were amused, though they did not show it to us. They led the way and, of course, went fast. I thought it must be around midnight when someone proposed our returning home. Dr. Palmer seemed glad to hear the words and being tired, we were all willing to follow the suggestion.

Nearing the house, we were amazed to see lights in the parlor so late and as we dragged our tired feet over the threshold, the clock pointed to nine, and Pa said, "Hand me the Testament; it is time for prayers."

When Brother Kim had passed his seventeenth birthday several months, the Confederacy made another call for men. Pa would have kept him at home until he was eighteen, but there were soldiers of his acquaintance going east as far as North Carolina and he thought it a good time for him to make the long journey. It was arranged that Brother Kim should visit in the homes of our relatives until he should be eighteen, old enough to enlist in the Confederate army.

Pa's hair turned white when Brother Kim went to war. This son had been the companion on long trips and hunts and was ever at his beck and call and had patiently suffered his fits of high temper and irritability. Yes, Brother Kim was a good boy. I have to this day his commentary on Proverbs. He wasn't fond of his studies, but he did love his Bible and faithfully memorized the passages assigned Sunday afternoons.

Pa always demanded the respect of the members of his household. I remember once, along about that time, Brother Kim said, "Honey, you and Harriet come on and go with me to the buzzard tree woods. Meet me at the back gate."

We looked at each other in astonishment, as he hurried off to get the cart and oxen hitched out near the barn, for Brother Kim seldom wanted us girls "tagging along" after him. We hopped into the cart behind him and soon learned that he was going after a load of pine knots. The day before, Pa had called him from a distance. He had answered "Sir," without getting Pa to hear him and he yelled out "Heigh-o!" That carried, but returned the punishment of Brother Kim's hauling fourteen loads of pine knots from the far field. We felt that this was a right severe punishment and willingly went to work to help him. Sue, Lute, and I surely enjoyed going with him to get the lightwood. The knots lay around in abundance over the rough ground and we had fun pitching them in the cart. We would pile them up while Brother Kim hauled them. All three of us almost forgot it was a task we had such fun. In two days, working at intervals, the fourteen loads were hauled. These pine knots were used to start fires and make light.

It was lonely after Brother Kim left for the east and we anxiously watched for the mail. Letters came as often as could be expected in war times. He stopped a short while with the soldiers in Sommerville and Memphis and then carried out the plan mapped by Pa to visit his relatives in North Carolina until he could join the army. When he reached North Carolina, he wrote of the good times he was having getting acquainted with his new kin and later of his life among the soldiers. He spent most of this time of waiting in Pa's sister Ann's home and wrote of the pretty young girls and of her sons in the army. Finally, a letter came saying he, too, had enlisted.

April 18, 1864. The boom of cannon sounded over towards Poison Springs![56] Now we felt like we were right in the midst of war. It was not long before soldiers came straggling up to the house. The first squad came through the kitchen and Aunt 'Riah said they picked from the mud and ate bread she had thrown to the ducks and ate raw dough from the tray before she could cook it, they were so hungry.

Two of the soldiers had been wounded in the arm and another in the head. I remember we scraped an old table cloth into lint with which to dress their wounds. We fed the hungry soldiers as best we could and for a while our house was a kind of hospital for some of them. Mr. Ivy and the Wilks brothers stayed several weeks, returning to their company when Shelby's army came to camp near us.

I have said that Mr. Wilks and Mr. Ivy, who had been wounded, stayed with us several weeks. All of us, from Pa to Nell, thought much of them. When Shelby was at home, Mr. Wilks came to see us on one occasion. When he entered the gate all went to meet him as though he were a brother. There was a young major in the parlor, whom no one had scarcely noticed. When we returned with our guest to the house, out he came, greeting him with, "My dear Ned, how glad I am to see you! How is your health?" "Very Well, thank you," replied Mr. Wilks and passed on by. The major told us many amusing anecdotes, but Mr. Wilks did not notice him further. Finally, when the major left, Mr. Wilks told us that he and the major had been friends and school mates, but after he was made a major he had never noticed him, though they had been thrown together often, until he saw how much we made of him. Sister Nannie said, "Officers cannot be too familiar with soldiers."

General Shelby and General Marmaduke, retreating before General Steele, camped for two weeks or more in our front grove. General Shelby had his headquarters in our office in the yard and General Marmaduke's headquarters were by the new crib, midway the grove. General Shelby had an uncle-in-law and other kin with him. Some of our soldier friends told us there were almost as many deadheads as regular soldiers on Shelby's staff.[57]

I don't remember how Colonel Greene looked but General Marmaduke was slender and had thin sandy hair and whiskers. He was very quiet and folks said he was single. General Shelby had a moustache and made himself pleasant to all. I think he was not as bald as General Marmaduke. I was but a child and thought both generals quite handsome.

They often sat on our front porch and seemed much amused at Pa's accounts of his deer hunts of which he was so fond. Once when the porch was full of illustrious guests, Aunt 'Riah rushed out saying, "Marster, I wish you'd send sum body to hist dat man off my kitchen table; he jest sets dar, meek as a lam', but evy time I tuns my back, er piece er chicken is gone." Of course the man was not found on the table when she returned to the kitchen, but afterwards two soldiers were kept on guard there, as well as several other places around the house.

One morning Pa called the guards to prayers. They said, "But Colonel Bullock, you had better let us watch while the others pray." But Pa replied, "No, you all come on to prayers." After breakfast we found that all the cloth that had been woven for our dresses had been cut from the loom. A neighbor told us that a soldier had brought her two yards of cloth from which to make him a shirt. That was about the length of the piece we had left in the loom and it answered to the same description.

One day Mr. Kim Jones invited General Shelby over to eat strawberries at his home and the invitation was graciously accepted. Mr. Jones had a large, well-furnished home with beautiful grounds surrounding it. His daughters had prepared quite a feast of lamb, pig, fowls, vegetables and a nice sugar cake to eat with the strawberries.

When all was ready, Mr. Jones sent Mr. Duff, his son-in-law, to conduct the guests to his home.[58] Two, three, four o'clock came without any sign of the visitors and when five o'clock drew near, in walked Mr. Duff alone, saying the general was asleep and he could not disturb him. Our family had strawberries from Mr. Jones's the next day for dinner, but General Shelby and his staff never dined there as I know of.

It was amusing to hear the ladies talk to General Shelby, whose soldiers were thought to be horse thieves and to take every good riding-horse they could find. At different times ladies and gentlemen would come to find their lost horses and General Shelby was always as polite to them as could be, but their horses were seldom found.

I remember Mrs. Al Green, a masculine assertive woman, who wanted her belongings. On her arrival she was invited into our parlor and when the general came in she told him her fine horse was supposed to be with his men and that if she could see anyone on him she would shoot him off. The general was all kindness and gave her an escort to help her find her horse, but the search was in vain. Sister Nannie said she supposed the horse was under cover before they left the house.

Then Ellen Phillips and her sister came.[59] They were pretty and well-pleasing to the eye. "Mother is a widow," said Ellen, "and that horse is her only support. I know if it is here, it is without your knowledge, but I hope you will let someone see if it can be found." I heard that Ellen and her sister rode a horse when she left.

After these generals had been encamped with us a few days, Colonel Greene[60] with his staff rode up to the gate and was directed to the blacksmith's shop back of the house for his headquarters.

We were then almost surrounded by soldiers. The children were told never to leave the house while they were camping near. We lived on a hill, with clear streams of water on three sides, and Pa had the underbrush cleared out, which made a large plot suited to camping ground.

I do not remember how Colonel Greene looked, nor do I remember any of his men. We knew many soldiers, for often twenty or thirty would eat supper with us, sit with the family until bedtime and then go to the woods to sleep. After staying with us two weeks or more, the whole division left. Pa had their camping grounds scraped and the refuse burned. There was so much meat and other refuse he was afraid it would cause sickness. The Negroes said it was nothing to see great hunks of beef thrown around in the tents, but I guess it was the slaughter pens that needed cleaning most. I remember seeing old harness thread, old clothing, and books. There I saw my first copy of Shakespeare's works. Sister Nannie was careful about what we read, therefore I hid it from her while I feasted upon the wonderful pages. One day she came upon me while I was reading it, and much to my surprise, she was delighted, encouraged me to continue reading it, and said she was sorry she had neglected getting more of the classics in our library.

As a child I was a great reader and Sister Nannie was careful about the kind of literature that reached our hands. I would hide, in the grape arbor or under my mattress, books that got into our hands through other ways than the church, which might be questioned and secretly I read with delight an ancient mythology and *Robinson Crusoe*. I was much surprised when she found them and seemed very pleased that I should read them.

About that time a new book was heatedly discussed by my elders, *Uncle Tom's Cabin*, by Harriet Beecher Stowe. Sister Kate wrote that she was highly entertained by the new novelette and thought the author such a fascinating writer most any Southerner could afford to receive her thrusts at slavery without offense, said she possessed such an insight of the human heart and delineated so minutely and clearly the varied thoughts and emotions and set forth her ideas in such a becoming dress that an attentive, thinking reader cannot fail to become interested, though their views on some essential points might differ. Sister Nannie liked the book too and read it to us children.

One Sunday morning Pa ordered the wagons to go over and bring the salt home. The (Confederate) government had employed our slaves to mine and bag the salt and paid Pa for this work with several bags of salt. We were greatly amazed that this work should be done on the Sabbath day, but Pa seemed so worried we were afraid to question. The next morning we were again surprised to see three horses tied at the front gate when we finished an early breakfast and wondered why Pa, Mr. Hicks, and Mr. Palmer should ride off in such a hurry. Mr. Hicks was sick and Mr. Palmer, who had buried his fourth brother the week before, had been confined to his bed in our home for several days. As they started, we heard Pa say, "We must go through the cane brake."

About nine o'clock that morning, twenty or thirty soldiers in uniforms of bright blue with bright trimmings turned in at the big gate. We knew at once they were Yankees and the mystery of the early morning was solved! How different these well-groomed soldiers looked from the ragged, half-starved Southern troops who had just left us!

All of our family gathered in Ma's room. Some of the soldiers hastened to the stables while others rushed into the yard and over the house, without any ceremony. One, who seemed to be the leader, called Gracie, a bright-looking colored girl, into the dairy and closed the door. After a few moments he stepped out and said, "All have escaped." The Yankees had learned of the Southern soldiers taking refuge with us, and had come to capture them.

At the front gate they had tied our horses, ready to be taken off. When Honey saw her little pony among them, she began to cry and to beg them not to take it away from her. On learning the cause of her tears, the lieutenant, who seemed to be a kind-hearted man and a gentleman, went to the gate and said, "Boys, that pony is too small for our use, don't take it from the little sissy." After it had been turned into the yard he advised Honey to have a pen built for it under her window. She did this, and there the pony stayed until the close of the war. This kind-hearted lieutenant gave Sister Nannie a letter of protection and told her if she would give it to any of the Northern soldiers, they would never molest her.

A fresh little upstart from a white mountain farm said something about freeing the slaves and Ma, crying, asked, "How shall our children be provided for if our Negroes are taken away?" "Put them chaps in the truck patch," he replied, with an air of superiority. At this remark, the lieutenant turned and gave him such a withering look he blushed and slouched off.[61]

One of the soldiers asked Ma for a ham, another asked for a turkey and she gave these graciously, from all outward appearance.

Aunt Patsy said some of the soldiers took her and the other slaves off and tried to persuade them to leave us, promising them a plenty of coffee and sugar. "We don't want none er yer coffee an' sugar, I tol 'um, we is got er plenty." Then she went on, "When dey axed me whar 'twuz, I sed, 'tis in de box, hind de do' an' when dey seed de rye an' de 'taters dey laf, an' I hilt up my head an' sed dat wuz de kin' we laks."

When the Yankee soldiers were ready to go, our colored men were called in from the fields to ride the horses to town. There was one mule, old Joe, which no one could get out of the stable. Finally one of the Negroes said that nobody but Jerry could ride Joe. Fourteen year old Jerry was called and with a proud, delighted laugh he mounted the fractious animal, which sprang out of the stable and galloped up the avenue at full speed. At the far gate the mule put his feet together and threw Jerry high into the air. When the boy remounted, the mule repeated the trick and walked off to eat grass. No one could get old Joe beyond the big gate. He and our pony Fanny started our crop the next year.

About this time Pa came back from leading the Southern soldiers to a place of safety. He told the Yankees he had never voted against the Union and they had no right to take his property and that he would go with them if they took his horses. When they left, he accompanied them.

Our hearts were heavy. What would they do with Pa? But these were war times and no sooner had night fallen than scouts from Shelby's army came and asked Ma for supplies. She gave them the smoke-house keys and they carried off a wagon nearly full of meat—all we had but two small middlings. They, also, tried in vain to get old Joe.

The next day Pa came riding up the avenue. Jerry ran to open the gate and we gathered around him as he dismounted and followed him to his seat on the porch to hear him relate his experiences of the past few hours. He said that when he reached Arkadelphia with the Yankees and his horses, General

Steele had just eaten dinner and appeared glad to see him, for he wanted advice about the best way to get down the river. He advised the route which he afterwards took. The General said, also, Pa was right about his horses and mules and gave him a note for eleven hundred dollars for them. He offered him a drink of whiskey, also, but Pa refused that.

When Pa had ridden a short distance out of Arkadelphia, he was surrounded by some of Shelby's scouts and taken to headquarters, now on Colonel Whittaker's plantation.[62] Fortunately, one of Pa's friends, Dr. Lewis Cooper, had charge of the plantation at that time and he spoke in his behalf. "To hear Dr. Cooper talk," said Pa, "one would have thought I had befriended most of the women and children made widows and orphans by the war, helped to supply with food most of the Southern army west of the Mississippi, and had given, in my two sons, the bravest soldiers of the east but that his son Billy had done most of the fighting in the war."[63]

General Shelby was so impressed with so loyal a citizen that he not only set him at liberty, but afterwards gave him a note for all the supplies the soldiers had taken during his absence.

Some of our neighbors were less fortunate and lost heavily. Mrs. Trigg, who lived nearby, said the Yankees tried to get everything they had.[64] They even took all of her husband's shirts. She went right to work to make him one out of an old piece of soiled goods she found. When she finished it she washed it and hung it out to dry. A thieving Yankee came back and got this one.

During the war, Mr. Scott kept the slaves at work and they made good crops. After harvest the cribs were filled overflowing with corn. From near and far people would come to buy, beg, or borrow from us when they were in need.

I remember one night about sun down, we heard cries of

distress over towards the big woods and someone was sent to learn the trouble. An old man near eighty and a young stripling of a girl, driving an ox cart, had lost the way and the cart was hitched in between trees so neither the old man or the girl could get it out. They lived between fifty and seventy-five miles away and on hearing that Pa had corn for sale, had started out to get some. They stayed a day or two until they were rested enough to undertake the return trip with a load of corn. To me they were a pitiful sight as they drove off.

6

From the first, Pa felt that the South was fighting a losing cause, that the Confederacy would not stand, and that in the end, the Negroes would go. Preparatory for this he had all our maids, except one, join the field hands and we were encouraged to learn to wait on ourselves and to carry on the housework. Aunt 'Riah and her scullion did the cooking and several women the washing.

Each of us had had a Negro girl at our beck and call. Emily was the name of mine. She tied my shoes, brushed my hair, hung up my clothes, saw that I always had my sunbonnet on when I went out of doors and seldom, without permission, ventured out of the sound of my voice. I loved the servants. So far as I ever saw, during the four years of the war (and as I sympathized with the Negroes they expressed themselves more freely before me than before others) I never heard any hint of rebellion. There was nothing but thorough loyalty to "Master" and their "white folks." They were dependent on us and we depended on them. There was no trouble until the matter was settled that they must be freed and then both white and colored united in claiming the freedom granted by the Proclamation of Emancipation; for slavery had bonds of servitude and responsibility for white people as well as for the Negroes.[65]

As I left home before the slaves, and entered upon new surroundings off at school, I did not feel so keenly the shift in our own domestic life, though hardships and sacrifices were experienced by all everywhere.

After Lee's surrender, the Negroes stayed on the rest of the year and a portion of the crop was allotted to them, the beginning of the independent life. This is what Tiny told me years after, "It seemed lak we had ter do sumpin' when we wuz free. Mammy, she married Uncle Wes Trigg an' went ter Mr. MacCallister's, fo' an' er half miles away an' stayed der one yer. Dat didn't seem nat'ul to her, so de nex' yer she car'd me back to de home place an' I been dar ever since. I want ter die dar. Aunt Patsy, Uncle Oscar and deir chilluns went ter Mr. Ausey Hunter's.[66] Aunt Riah and Uncle Billy stayed on a year or two an' den went ter Mr. Pratt's. All de others went ter different places."

In the early spring of '65, when the Yankees going north had passed us, Miss Mary Cooper, the teacher who had refugeed at home during the war and been our teacher, said now the way would be clear for her to return home in Staunton, Virginia. But before going she wished to stop with her old friends in Tulip, where she had been teaching when the war broke up the school in which she had been teaching. It had been arranged that my younger sister Lute and I should attend the Female Academy there under the management of Rev. and Mrs. Edward Barcus.[67] Near the outbreak of the war the building had been burned and now these good people were trying to reestablish and carry on the work of the much needed institution in their home and in the music hall which they had formerly had charge of.

Our preparations for going off to school were very simple. All of our clothes were home woven, except my Sunday dress, which was made from one of Sister Nannie's old ones, and one for Lute, made from one of Honey's old ones. Pa was to pay a part of our board with provisions. On the day appointed for us to leave, the oxen, four in number, were hitched to a wagon. Two hundred pounds of meat, a five gallon jar of lard, bags of meal and of flour, a trunk for each of us girls and for Miss Mary, along with other luggage, were piled on. Then Miss Mary, Lute and I crawled in, and after taking our seats on covered bags of meal, we drove off in grand style. The whole family, from little Sarah Palmer, in her nurse's arms, to Pa, were at the gate to see us off and waved adieus as we slowly drove down the long avenue to the big gate and out into the main road.

This was rough and muddy and did not improve as we went along. After we had gone ten or twelve miles a trunk toppled over, crushing the jar of lard. We were puzzled to know what to do until we spied a log cabin in the distance. Miss Mary said we girls could go there and try to borrow a vessel in which to save the lard. The house looked poor, indeed, to us and no one was in sight. It was a long time before we saw any sign of life, save a thin smoke curling from the chimney. A Negro girl finally responded to our knock and asked us into the living room. There, lying on the trundle bed, was a lady, moaning with toothache and several little children stood around staring at her.

After we had become accustomed to the dim light, I recognized the sufferer as a former neighbor, Miss Betty Littlejohn, who had run away from school several years before and married Bob Hunter. His family was of the best in the land and her father was a Methodist preacher.[68] Miss Betty had been the prettiest, daintiest girl who attended the old Manchester church and was reared in a beautiful home, surrounded by the comforts of the times. There had been some objection to the marriage; they had become estranged from their people and were now nobly suffering, as thousands of others, the adversities of war. She lent us the bucket in which most of the lard was saved, and on we drove.

About night we reached the Barcus home and I met for the first time the family which afterwards became so closely associated with ours. Mr. Barcus was a handsome man, with a Grecian nose and beautiful dark eyes with expressions varying with his conversation. At all times he looked as neat as a pin. Mrs. Barcus had gray-green eyes that were ever laughing. I never saw tears in them but once and that was when Mr. Barcus teased her about denying him cream in order to have it to give to a poor neighbor.

There were several children in the Barcus family, besides the boarding pupils. Lute and I soon found friends among the girls, but especially were we drawn to Mary, the oldest daughter, who was always refined, genteel, and sweet, as well as good natured. Though we had not met the Barcus family, we were not strangers in Tulip, which was at that time a health resort, and Sister Nannie had taken me there with her as she was recovering from a spell of fever. She would not leave me at home because I played so much with the little Negroes. I then found numerous companions among the neighbors. What a time we boys and girls had! Sister Nannie said I wore out thirteen dresses and several pairs of shoes, so she took me home because I had nothing to wear in company. Many of these old acquaintances were still in town and some of the girls were in school.

After devoting so much of the home to the accommodation of the school, there was no spare sitting room. Company was entertained in Mrs. Barcus's bedroom. This arrangement was rather mortifying to us girls and on one occasion furnished a rather amusing experience. One evening some young men, wealthy cousins of ours, called and when Mrs. Barcus was told who was at the door, she gave the trundle bed a kick, which sent it under the high bed. This must have produced a general bumping of heads, for as the young men entered, the three boys began to howl and kept this up during a most embarrassing greeting. But Mrs. Barcus, in her calm, unperturbed way, restored order and led us out into such pleasant conversation, we forgot the humiliating situation and spent a pleasant evening around the fireside.

Family worship was regularly conducted in the Barcus home. When Mr. Barcus was away, his wife took his place at the altar. On one of these occasions my attention during the prayer was diverted by a slight noise at the hearth and I opened my eyes. Mrs. Barcus, holding the baby in one arm, and taking the frying pan from the fire with her free hand, was praying on in unbroken tones, eloquently thanking our Heavenly Father for his blessings. Had I been more reverent, and not opened my eyes, I would never have known how the chicken escaped a burning.

She has ever been a wonder to me! Her servants were poor and often she had none; Mr. Barcus not only taught music in the school, but was much of the time away from home, meeting his preaching appointments. For a time she was without a cook stove and the cooking was done on the kitchen fireplace.

In the fall when the potatoes were dug we girls asked if we might have the ones we could glean from the field. Mr. Barcus gave his consent, but when we stored them in boxes under our beds, Mrs. Barcus was very mortified at this suggestion that her table was not abundantly supplied with food. We had so much fun roasting those potatoes in our rooms at night, during study hour.

Once when we had company I was served a tempting piece of chicken, which I laid on the side of my plate, saving the best for the last. Seeing the dish empty, she reached over, took the piece from my plate and gave it to one of the children, as she said, "Harriet does not seem to want her piece." To this day I have longed for that piece of chicken!

Rules about going with boys were strict; and this was hard on us who had friends in town, but I always tried to obey the regulations. Sometimes the boys would hide behind trees or shrubbery and as the row of school girls passed, one would slip in between two girls and walk along with the one of his choice, undetected. This, of course, was a prank played at night.

One delightful afternoon Mrs. Barcus told us we might go out alone to the site of the old Institute, which had been burned, if we would promise not to speak to any young man whom we might meet. As we turned from the highway into the path leading to the ruins, in the distance we spied some men on horse back. To avoid embarrassment, and at the same time keep our promise, we ran and hid in the standing chimneys of the destroyed building. When the young men reached the place where we turned from the road, we heard one say, "I know I saw them here; how could they have gotten away so quickly without our seeing them?" They came near enough the ruins to make a casual survey of the place without finding us. When they had gone some time, cautiously we slipped out and walked slowly home, laughing at the way we had escaped from the riders. But at the sight of Mrs. Barcus our mirth and laughter ceased. She met us at the gate and gently broke the news of Brother Kim's death. The young men were soldiers returning home from the war, sent by to let us know. Encamped somewhere in eastern North Carolina, he had contracted fever and died among strangers. In his unconscious raving he had called, "Sister Nannie, Sister Nannie!"

That was all we could learn. We hoped, somehow, it was a mistake, that the victim of that case of fever was another soldier. True, it had been a long time since we had had news of him, but we were stunned beyond the realization of the worst. It could not be that merry-hearted Brother Kim would never again join us in our romps and frolics, that he would never ride off with Pa, going hunting. Surely our North Carolina relatives would have known something about him and written!

The days dragged slowly by and we welcomed vacation. It was arranged that we get home in time to meet Brother Tom on his return from the army, after Lee's surrender. He rode up behind our cart just as we were about to turn in at the avenue. I shall never forget how handsome he looked and just as we were about to stop the cart and tumble out for a greeting, he gave his horse a cut with the switch and scampered off down the drive toward the house, laughing as victor of the race.

However, we knew it was to hide his grief. It was hard for him to come home without Brother Kim. He shrank from talk about the war, seemed to wish to forget the horrors and suffering of the past four years. We knew he could find out nothing about Brother Kim, from whom he had been separated, and only knew, as did we, that his body lay somewhere in an unmarked soldier's grave.

Pa was now old and delicate; he could not go in search of

the body himself, but sent others who were searching for the remains of their loved ones. Among these searchers was his friend, Mr. MacCallum, and it was through his influence that he received this letter many months later.

Mill Grove, Harnett Co., N.C.
May 7, 1867

Col. Chas Bullock
Cassamassa, Ark.

Dear Sir:

Mr. I. B. MacCallum, from your place, inquired of me the whereabouts of your son's grave. I have ascertained, and report to you.

He died at Mr. John Robert Taylor's home on the road from Fayetteville to Raleigh, sixteen miles north of Fayetteville, and is buried in his field. He died the day the Northern army left, and necessarily buried in his blanket—no coffin. The Confederate dead have all been exhumed and buried in a cemetery on the battlefield, which we expect to enclose, and if we can raise funds, will have a monument.

If it is your wish to have the remains of your son removed to this place, let me know as soon as possible and it will be attended to. Any service I can render you I will cheerfully do.

Respectfully,
D. D. MacBride

I know Pa sent what he thought to be enough money to have Brother Kim's body nicely buried and a monument above his grave. But his wishes were never carried out. We suppose his body was moved to the Confederate cemetery and is among those to whom a monument was erected, bearing the inscription, "To the Unknown Dead."

As for the other boys in the neighborhood there were the

Harrises, Joneses, Littlejohns, and many others. Along about that time I liked Sammy Colburn better than any of the others. After we went home from Tulip on our vacation he came down to see us. Rambling over the plantation was always one of our favorite passtimes and we girls took Sammy out for a walk. At one point we came near enough the public road to spy in a distance a long train of covered wagons going west. I ran, and jumping up on a fence nearby, screamed to the top of my voice, "Hi there, bank o' wagons! Hi there, bank o' wagons."

"Why, Miss Harriet," said Sammy, "I wouldn't do that."

"We always say that when we see wagoners pass," I replied, "We don't mean anything."

"But think of them. That is rude," he reproved. I thought of Sammy and never hailed passers again. I was greatly disappointed when I heard he was going to be a Methodist preacher.

Not long after that I went on a visit to Wilson Ella MacCaskill. Wilson Ella's mother, Aunt Becky, as we called her, let us do pretty much as we pleased, as long as we had harmless fun. We were big girls, but barefooted we roamed the garden and nearby fields. About ten o'clock one morning we sat perched on top of the grape arbor and were laughing and singing as we swayed among the vines. One of us looked up and saw in the distance the young preacher Sammy on horseback. Down we dropped, scampered behind the shrubbery, slipped in the back door, reached our room and began primping to look our prettiest. Painting and chalking were in style then too, but we had no paint and used corn starch for powder. We had not gone through the war, however, without learning substitutes for cosmetics as well as for other things. Pokeberries hung in abundance from the bushes in almost every fence corner and we had a supply of these on our dresser. With great care, most deftly we painted our cheeks.

How natural! How beautiful, we told each other we looked. Highly satisfied with ourselves we went down to the parlor and gaily chatted the preacher. When dinner was announced and we had taken our seats at the table, the Indian girl who served walked in with her face boldly streaked and smeared all over with pokeberries. All of us began to laugh and Aunt Becky asked, "Why, Mol, what did you streak your face up with pokeberries for?" "Miss Harriet and Miss Wilson Ella did," she said, pointing an accusing finger at us; "pretty, very pretty." We blushed beneath the coloring and were much embarrassed during the rest of the meal. As soon as possible we washed our faces and again gave each other the assurance, "Yes, it is all off. Just chalk your face now, and it will look all right."

Sammy died of fever a few years later, I heard. I don't think he ever married. But I did not say I was his sweetheart. I said he was mine, then. He had left Tulip when we went back to school there in the fall.

Did we girls ever get into mischief? Yes, I suspect we gave Mr. and Mrs. Barcus more trouble than we ever knew; but our fun was usually harmless. We would maneuver all kinds of ways to talk to the boys we liked and it was one of the boys' favorite tricks to drop in our line as we marched from church and walk with the girls they liked best. There were some boys Mrs. Barcus did not seem to mind our going with and would sometimes invite them to see us but somehow we did not enjoy the company of her selections.

One day a crowd of rather wild fellows passed and seeing a group of girls on the lawn, began throwing them apples they had stolen from a nearby orchard. In the midst of that sport, who should come up but Mr. Barcus. The boys quickly disappeared and Mr. Barcus gathered up all the apples from the girls and threw them to the pigs. Cruel punishment, we thought!

I did not realize then what a struggle Mr. and Mrs. Barcus were having to keep the Academy going. They were good teachers and made home pleasant for us. Mrs. Barcus was mother, teacher and housekeeper. And he was teacher, tailor and preacher. He fashioned his own clothes which always fitted him beautifully.

On almost every Friday afternoon he would leave to go on his circuit to the churches of his charge and would not return until Monday and then he was all tired out. I remember hearing him say he had collected from the churches only forty-five dollars during the whole quarter and little more from the patrons of the school.

Time and again he would say to his wife, "Mary, we cannot go on this way. The work is entirely too much for you. I believe I will give it all up for I know I can make a good living for my family at the tailor's trade, or at almost any other occupation than preaching." "Oh, no," she would reply, "the Lord will provide; you preach the Lord. We may be perplexed, but not cast down."

He took the advice of his good wife and kept on preaching, but a few years afterwards, moved to Texas where he "died in harness" at a ripe old age.

Lute and I did not finish out our second term there. She would go with Mary to drive up the calves in the mornings while the dew was still on the grass. This did not hurt Mary, for she was bare footed. Lute, who was older, had on shoes and she did not dry her feet on returning to the house. Perhaps it was in this way that she contracted a cough which would not be cured in spite of the numerous remedies Mrs. Barcus tried.

Lute grew so thin I wrote home and told Pa about her lingering cough. He came up to see about us. I don't think he intended to take us home, for he brought with him a lot of provisions, but the message of my letter was verified by Lute's startling appearance and both of us went home, for I felt that I could not stay without her.

As the weather grew warmer, Lute got well of her cough that I had feared was caused by consumption, as we called tuberculosis.

At the academy I had been a boarder and a student; now I had to share the house work with my other sisters and I still felt keenly the change at home after the slaves were gone. Aunt 'Riah and the other servants who had moved away were sorely missed. Cooking, washing, housecleaning and attending to the milk were not easy for us girls. Sister Nannie bought a washing machine, but after her first attempt at laundry she stayed in bed a week. Being unaccustomed to hard work, we did not know how to go about it. This made us irritable and fussy, all except Honey. I remember her as always being patient and sweet tempered, helping me out of many a trouble.

Neither did things on the plantation go on so smoothly. Mr. Scott, who was still with us, could not get hands to plant and work the crops and the way had not been opened for Pa to take his cotton, accumulated during the war, down to New Orleans to sell. And the new system of labor was a problem. Once a hand spoke impertinently to Pa, who picked up a hoe and gave him a blow on the head. The Negro, though not seriously hurt, was infuriated and took the matter to court. The case was decided in favor of the Negro and Pa had another lesson in the treatment of freedmen.

We had not been at home long before Mr. Barcus made us a visit. From the porch Pa saw him drive in at the front gate and was immediately taken so ill he had to go to bed. He had not sold his cotton and knew that Mr. Barcus had come to collect our board and tuition. After having greeted all the family and rested a while from his long journey, he was invited in to see Pa. I suppose he would have said nothing about the money to Pa while he was sick, but Pa asked him the amount of the bill. Mr. Barcus said it was a hundred dollars. Immediately, Pa began to improve and was able, after a short time, to get up and entertain his guest in his usual hospitable manner. The idea of not being able to pay for our board and tuition in full, when called for, had upset his digestion to the extent he was really sick. When he learned the amount was so small, his constitution responded to his mental attitude toward relieved anxiety.

Everything seemed so changed by this time. Many of the old servants had gone and what work went on was under the reign of confusion. Pa had tried to prepare us for it, but such a change as was produced by freeing of the slaves had to be worked out by actual necessity.

Pa got a good price for his cotton and did not suffer the harsh reverses that some did. He spent, however, freely and gave to many in need. I know he bought several tracts of cheap land in the nearby counties and houses in Arkadelphia, besides being largely interested in the drug store where Brother Tom worked and where Dr. Palmer had his office.[69] The Palmers had now moved from Sylvan Home to town.

7

It was about this time that Miss Mary Connerly, a young woman from the North came to Arkadelphia and established a school for girls.[70] She used the building of the old Baptist Institute, and here, making our home with Sister Anna Booker, Lute and I continued our studies in the fall after leaving Tulip.

Miss Connerly was a member of the Presbyterian Church and though not obtrusive, was ever willing to give a helping hand to work for the advancement of the cause of Christ. Much of this was through contact with pupils of her school, as she labored to instill right principles in them. I thought I had ever lived with good people, but she taught me honesty on a higher plane than I had learned before.

In decorating the church for an entertainment, I tore the counterpane borrowed from my sister. She quietly darned the torn places nicely, saying that her being my sister gave me no right to abuse her things and that as supervisor of the decorations, she was responsible for the condition of the counterpanes when they were returned. I remember, also, she said a teacher had no right to give a pupil a perfect grade unless she did perfect work.

One holiday we had a Sunday School entertainment, followed by a picnic, and the school had to march in a body to the grounds. There was one little girl among us, very poorly dressed, with whom none of the others wished to march, because her people were not considered of the first class. Miss Connerly would not rest until she had her happily mated with me and the march to the picnic was a success, for I had been made to feel that I was honored in being asked to perform this favor.

Though we boarded with our sister, we had to keep regulations about going with young men. At every party we had there were about three boys to every girl, for after the war, the young men from the east continued to seek their fortune in the west and Arkadelphia was far enough in that direction to catch a goodly number of these travelers.

I had my beaux and sweethearts and it would be hard for any of you to beat me at primping. I painted my cheeks, powdered with swans' down, and put belladonna in my eyes to make them sparkle. At one time I cut my hair short enough to hang in ringlets and later I wore artificial braids and curls. I remember I gave twenty dollars for one braid.

There were the Stuarts, Joneses, Butlers, Strongs, Harrises, Colburns and numerous others. At one time Johnny Singleton was a favorite of mine, but he was not a beau, for he was engaged to another girl. He boarded near our home and often dropped in to see us. I would urge him to go to prayer meeting, but he followed his crowd, while asking me to pray for him. He knew I was interested in his leading a good life and girls do have so much to do with the way a man lives! After a while he was taken with fever and on his death bed sent for me to pray for him. Sister Anna took me over and I was so glad I went. He said he was trusting in the Saviour and was unafraid to die. He asked his sister to give me a little ring after his death. This I kept for a long time. Here is his picture. You may laugh at his floppit trousers and sleeves, his unbuttoned vest and narrow string tie, but those are what they wore in those days.

I attended Pa's church and Governor Flanagan was my Sunday School teacher. He was a good one, too. I used to visit in his home and was very fond of his children. On one of these occasions I remember the Governor had promised to pay his little son Duncan a cent a hundred for all the flies he would kill. Duncan filled a glass nearly full of soapy water and on this was placed a piece of pasteboard with a hole in the center. Molasses was smeared on the side next to the water. When the flies crept through the hole for a feast on molasses they were drowned. Duncan agreed to pay his little sister Laura half the money if she would count the flies.

Brother Tom came in from the store one day with the news that he had received a letter from one of our cousins in North Carolina, Nat Daniel, a druggist whom he had met while in the army, asking if he might stop over and make us a visit while on his way to join his brother, Venable, a druggist in San Marcos, Texas. His journey lay through Arkadelphia and he hoped to stop over there and see something of our family. All of us were very enthusiastic over the prospect of a visit from this cousin, Pa's nephew.[71]

It was a pleasant afternoon in February, and some time later our family was to gather on the front veranda to enjoy the sunshine, when Brother Tom, a little earlier than usual, came in from the store. With him was a stranger, but as soon as Brother Tom saw us he called, "Here is Nat. He made better connections than he expected." He was not very tall, but had a graceful soldierly bearing and was handsome and neatly dressed. The merry twinkle in his black eyes and his kindly smile won a place in the hearts of us all. He kissed Lute, but I was too old for kisses from even a strange cousin and the rules of school forbade my joining him and Lute in a drive that afternoon. The town boys said our cousin from the east would soon win the hearts of all the girls and they would be left out in the cold.

As Cousin Nat had studied pharmacy while in college in Charlotte before the war, and another clerk was needed in our drug store, he was induced to surrender his plan of going to Texas for a position offered him in Arkadelphia. He soon filled a large place in our social circle. I was just a school girl and he made a confidante of me, relating little interesting instances about his life back home and telling the amusing daily happenings, so we became good friends and indeed, he did befriend me in my studies. Miss Connerly especially emphasized English, putting great stress on correct reading and spelling. Cousin Nat would call out the words for me to spell when I was preparing my lesson and mark the ones I missed. I remember once after some entertainment in the evening we all missed the lesson the next morning and Miss Connerly threw the book down and left the room. I know she had been greatly worried by something else to appear so impatient with us, for she was long-suffering and forbearing, usually. A Northerner and a Yankee had much in those times to endure among us hotheaded Southerners.

Miss Connerly was a beautiful reader and she believed in giving short lessons which she required us to learn well, regarding with great correctness the pronunciation, the enunciation, and the punctuation. Here Cousin Nat would help me, too, and I liked so much to hear him read the declamations and orations so numerous in our readers of that time.

I surely had been taught little self control. One day we had coconut pudding for dinner and of this I was specially fond. I ate enough to make me sick, but returned to school and went to recitations. When my turn for reading came, I could not call the words right and burst out crying. I was sent from the room, of course, and while I still like coconut pudding, it was a long time before I could enjoy it so much as before.

One weekend, Sister Nannie had us all out home for a party. Cousin Nat was among the young men invited from town. On our arrival, we found the house beautifully decorated and the dining table amply provided with fruits, cakes and confectionaries, all in readiness for the feast. A variety of games had been prepared and we had a wonderful time. Pa never allowed us to dance, but we played all sorts of active games. Someone introduced a new game which we liked very much and enjoyed stepping around to the music. Pa came to the door while we were in the midst of it and gave a long look, then turned around saying, "Ugh," and went to his room. He told us afterwards we were dancing the "Ol' Virginia Reel," but didn't seem to know it, so he did not break us up.

I found out later that someone had told Sister Nannie I was making myself a goose about Cousin Nat and she had planned the party to throw us together where she could see if this were true. When I asked her about it, she said I certainly did not give him any undue attention and seemed more interested in other boys, but that he did stay at my heels whenever he could.

And didn't I tell you that your grandpa never allowed us to bring cards in the house. Cousin Nat told me long afterwards that he brought a pack with him, but when he found that Pa did not allow us to play, he hid them in the loft of the weaver's room and never saw them again. He did not play with the other boys in Arkadelphia.

Miss Connerly's commencements were called examinations and they did justice to that name. On these occasions the hall was packed. That year they had a play called "The Queen of the Fairies," and I was the queen. All the girls were dressed beautifully and I felt so grand as I presided over them and had them do my bidding. Then we had the spelling "Bee," perhaps the feature of greatest interest. When time for our examination in mathematics came, I was given a long example of partial payments to work at the blackboard. As I neared the end, I saw the answer would not come out right. I had made a mistake. Fortunately, this same example had given me trouble before and I remembered the answer. Placing myself between the work and the people, I put down the answer and from memory worked the example backwards until the mistake was corrected. When I stood aside, my neat, accurate work received much commendation, but no one knew how near I came to failing completely.

Lute and I went to school in Arkadelphia two years. We were then thought to be ready for college. After considerable family discussion and some correspondence with those whom we deemed authorities on the subject of colleges, it was decided that we should go to one in Florence, Alabama, entering the next fall.

But now letters came from my sisters in Tennessee urging me to visit them. Sister Fanny lived in Sommerville and Sister Kate lived on the large Taylor plantation near that town. All of my older sisters had been to Grandma Shaperds, near Dancyville and had attended school in Sommerville. Honey especially had told me about the good times she had had there, so I was delighted to seize the opportunity of this trip which Pa offered. It would be on the way to Florence and he and Lute could come by there with me.

If I had known there was a plot behind it all, things might have been different, but I was all unconscious that the home folks were sending me away from Cousin Nat to prevent my marrying a first cousin. Not that they objected to him personally, for they loved him dearly and admired and respected him. But my elders knew that back east there had been frequent intermarriages in the past generations of Bullocks and that the continuation of this might prove unfortunate. If they had let the matter alone, no doubt Cousin Nat and I would have quarreled and fallen out; but as it was, I read my Bible through to see if I could find anything in it to forbid such a marriage, for I had such marriages questioned in my presence, though there was no open opposition to our friendship. If it is forbidden, I did not find it and haven't to this day though I have read my Bible through more than forty times.

8

The journey out was made in company with some of Pa's friends, in whose care I was placed. It was a thrilling experience. I had never been on a steamer like the one on which we traveled up the Mississippi to Memphis and all summer I had a grand time visiting in the homes of my two sisters and their friends, where there were parties, dinings and picnics where I rapidly made friends with the young people of their social circles.[72]

By the time the letter came saying that Pa and Lute would soon come by to take me to college in Florence, Sister Kate had influenced me not to go to college. She said Pa was getting old, had recently lost heavily in business, and being in feeble health, was not able to stand the financial strain our expenses would incur. So before they reached there, I had promised to teach in the neighborhood school and live with Sister Kate, so they went on to Florence without me. I was greatly distressed about not going to college but I had the comfort that I would not inflict a great burden of debt on Pa and that I could make my own expenses while living with Sister Kate.

The school was small and easy to teach and home life was most pleasant. Cousin Sam (as I called Sister Kate's husband, for the Taylors were from Virginia and distantly related to us) and Sister Kate lived at his father's home with him and his widowed daughter, Cousin Mary Taylor Reid. The latter kept house and I suppose she was responsible for its being "glittering and spotless like heaben," as one of the old servants described the home. She was a remarkable person and could accomplish more with less commotion than anyone I ever saw.

Uncle Edmund had family prayers three times a day, just like Pa did, and three times a day, after each meal, he would go in the parlor and engage in prayer and if any differences should arise as to cause a quarrel between the brothers, Uncle Edmund would quietly resort to his place of prayer until peace was restored.

Uncle Edmund was highly respected and much beloved, not only by his family, but by a wide circle of neighbors and friends, though at times he was very plain spoken. His sayings were often a source of much amusement to us who knew the well meaning of his great loving heart. At one of our church meetings the sermon was preached by a young man just entering the ministry. After the song following the sermon, Uncle Edmund arose and addressing the older minister, said, "This boy has told us all he knows, now you preach us a sermon."

One day at dinner Uncle Edmund rose to carve the fowl at the head of the table. While he was standing, a young man sitting next to him thoughtlessly put his foot on a round of Uncle Edmund's chair and pushed it back. When the latter resumed his seat the edge of the chair just saved him from a fall. With suppressed heat he settled in place and turning to the maid said, "Gal, go bring this man something to put his foot on."

Occasional letters came from home telling of changes in

family and community life which I could not realize would ever be. The drug store in Arkadelphia had failed. Dr. Palmer and Sister Anna had moved from Arkadelphia to Hempstead County [——] miles away, where Pa had bought up land in a promising community for a young doctor's practice.[73] Brother Tom said he could not work in the store and attend the farm, which needed him, as Pa was getting too old and feeble to manage it. He was also paying attention to Mr. Barcus's young daughter Mary, an old schoolmate.

Cousin Nat had a long spell of fever and had gone out to Sylvan Home to stay until he was strong enough to return to work in the store. He wrote to me occasionally. Sister Mary Helen and Judge Cross's nephew, Homer Cross, were married.[74]

I came in from school one afternoon when I had been in Tennessee nearly two years and found Uncle Edmund crying. "What is the matter, Uncle Edmund?" I asked, "Come here, Honey," he replied, "I have something to tell you." When I was seated near, he laid his hand over my shoulder and continued in broken tones, "My own grandchild is yonder paying board and Madam's sister is here living on me. Don't you think it is a shame."

"I certainly do," I sympathized. Then I gathered that he had just received a letter telling of one of his granddaughters, an orphan, who for some reason wished to move from her guardian's home and live somewhere that she had to pay board. This made Uncle Edmund very miserable.

I thought it was so funny, for I was "Madam's sister," that I told Sister Kate, who in turn burst out crying. I couldn't see why, for I knew Uncle Edmund was very fond of me and did not mean that he thought I was an extra expense, but being old and childish, he misunderstood the conditions which caused his granddaughter to pay board. Sister Kate, however, never looked at it in that way. She was deeply hurt. The next year she moved to the office in the yard to live and after my school closed in the spring of seventy I returned to Arkansas.

(While in Tennessee) I spent many weekends and a part of my summer vacations with Sister Fanny Dickinson. Many of my letters would be sent to her home before reaching me and she, hungry for home news, often opened and read them, though I asked her to wait until I had seen them first. One day as I came in from school, I was greeted by one of my sisters with the news that I had a letter from home which she had opened and read. Before she could remonstrate, I walked to the fire and laid the letter on a bed of glowing coals. This showed my sisters how deeply I felt about my rights to open my mail first and they never opened another letter of mine. Fortunately, that letter was from Cousin Nat and Sister had gotten the home news. "Why, Harriet, you have not read your letter," she said. "You have and there is no need for me to," I replied and quickly left the room.

That must have been one of the family letters Cousin Nat (your Pa) wrote me. He usually wrote me two in one enve-lope—one for myself, so marked that I could quickly hide it if received when I was in the presence of the others and read it alone, and another that I could read to the family. You see why I was very solicitous about my mail. My sisters were also keen to have news from home. I have tried to teach you children the sacredness of a sealed letter. You can see I had in the bottom of my heart a real reason for not wishing my letters to be opened.

While I was in the Taylor family there was one of those changes that sooner or later come to all homes. Cousin Mary Reid, the widowed sister, laid down her work as housekeeper for her family and married Mr. Jefferson, a fine wealthy widower, who had been for some time seeking her hand. He had a son and a daughter and Cousin Mary had a daughter. Both of the girls were at Staunton, Va. at the time of the marriage and I sent each of them a box of the wedding supper. I knew the separate box would please them more. Sister Kate then moved back from the office to the house and took Cousin Mary's place.

The son, Johnny Jefferson, lived with his father for some time and then ran off with a show. I never heard from him afterwards. I hope he came back all right after I left Tennessee. Many boys run away from home in the early teens. I remember his father would not allow him to eat butter and molasses on the same piece of bread. Each was considered sufficient relish. That seemed strange to me, for we had always eaten both, if we liked.

9

I had a delightful trip home and stopped in Little Rock to visit my old friends, the Pattons, who had moved there from Arkadelphia when the Blind Institute was moved. When I reached Arkadelphia, there were a number of old friends to welcome me. Among them was Cousin Nat.

He lingered after the gathering and it was then that I fully realized that he cared so much for me—so much that I was willing to admit that he had long held the first place in my affection. I had fought the fact by seeking and accepting attention from other boys; but now, happy in my trust in him, accepting their attention was merely to deceive the gossipers.

You cannot imagine how appalled I was at the changes two years had wrought at Sylvan Home. Pa and Ma had aged so much. The younger children—Mat, Nell and Charlie—had grown almost beyond my recognition. Aunt 'Riah and most of the other servants had moved away. My sisters were trying to carry on the housework: milking, cooking, washing and ironing. The cotton crop had suffered the drought and was small in comparison, from that cause as well as from a lack of labor.

Once sister Nannie tried to lead us in picking it. Again she was made sick. The servant problem had not been so great in Tennessee.

But we had our amusements in the way of parties and picnics. Cousin Nat's health was too bad to stand the confinement of the store, so he arranged with Pa to stay on and help with the work around the place. Pa kept up his rule of prayers and bedtime between nine and ten o'clock. Sometimes the boys would say good night and leave the parlor when they sensed it was nearing Pa's bedtime hour and we would keep quiet in the parlor, awaiting their return through the open window, after we thought he was asleep. This was group frolic and not enjoyed so often, but after the boys had ridden eight miles to see us, we thought they should have more time of our company.

Brother Tom would stay out late sometimes, too. Honey would always sit up to kiss him good night. She had heard he had been going with some of the lively crowd, but she had no need to fear about him. He was soon to be the groom, claiming much beloved Mary Barcus as a bride.

That summer, when time came for the annual camp meeting, Pa refused to let Sister Nannie and the other girls attend. She was surely "put out." She could not understand why Pa could not let them go; he had always taken such an interest in the camp meetings. When for some time I had heard her lamenting his denial, I said, "Sister Nannie, I can get Pa to let you go." "So see what you can do with him!" she exclaimed. Off I set, and soon found Pa. "Sister Nannie wants so much to go to camp meeting, Pa," I said, "you don't care if she goes, do you?" Wrathfully, he stormed, "Tell her to go if she is bound to go!" Returning to Sister Nannie, I announced that Pa said she could go. I did not tell her how he had given consent. "I knew the Lord would provide a way," she fervently exclaimed and hastily made preparations to leave for camp meeting grounds.

A few days later she returned and reported a great revival and wonderful spiritual feast. But she had not been home long before she went to bed and we sent for our family physician. He pronounced hers a case of typhoid fever, contracted, as were many others in his practice, from the water used at the camp meeting grounds. Pa's objection to her attending the meeting was owing to his having heard of typhoid cases in that section, but not being sure of their origin, and not willing to put out a false report as would interfere with the meeting, he had not given his reason for asking us to stay away.

For days Sister Nannie lingered at Death's door, so ill she would not lift a hand and was allowed as nourishment only the whey from buttermilk. Fortunately, another doctor was called in consultation and he said she was being starved to death. When she was given chicken broth and other suitable food, she began to recover and was well enough to attend Brother Tom and Sister Mary's wedding reception.

This was a grand affair. Brother Tom and the Barcus family were popular in that section of the state. Friends from Tulip, Camden, Arkadelphia and the surrounding country were sent invitations to the reception. We sent for Aunt 'Riah, our old cook, who had moved to a nearby plantation. Although the feeble, worn out servant was sick, and instead of being able to practice her former skills had to be nursed and so was a care instead of a help, preparations went on. The poor old darky went blind before she died—I suppose she injured her eyes with long cooking for us over the fire.

The house and surroundings were spick and span from the garret to the big front gate, half a mile away. Food for fifty people was prepared. At the foot of the table was a whole roasted pig with an apple in its mouth; the center piece was a pyramid formed of different colors of jelly and garnished with sprays of flowers. And on each side of this was another smaller pyramid of golden butter, printed and finished at the crest with butter curls. The bride's cake was an immense one, beautifully iced and decorated with many colors of icing flowers. Other meats and sweets were provided in abundance.

The bride and the groom with their attendants arrived but hours went by without the others. Supper was served and the evening was veiled with disappointment. Why didn't the other guests arrive? Some days later the invitations addressed to them were found in the pocket of an old coat, where they had been put when given to someone to be mailed. The man had changed his coat and forgotten the invitations. The friends who did not get their bidding to the reception felt as much slighted as we were disappointed.

Mary came to live with us and she was so sweet and thoughtful of us all. But it was not long before Sue went up to stay with Sister Anna in Hempstead County and teach her children in connection with the public school.

And Cousin Nat had his call away too. One day Cousin Nat received a letter from home telling him that his mother needed him to help look after the plantation. His health was delicate and while he was sick he had put all he had in the plantation to save it for his mother. Now it seemed that his interests and his mother's happiness called him back home. He thought, too, he might get stronger by leaving the river bottoms of Arkansas, where he had contracted malaria. Immediately he made preparations for leaving. Everyone seemed sad to see him go. He was not prepared to take me with him, neither was I prepared to go. It was behind the dining room door that he said the last hasty goodbye and I joined the others to wave farewell as he drove off.

In December he wrote me that he was coming back to take me out to North Carolina with him. I had by then started my trousseau. Pa gave me a hundred dollars more and I had everything ready by the time he arrived in January. The one thing that troubled me most was that Honey was away and I could not see her before going so far away.

Cousin Nat had written me that the times in the east were equally as hard since the war as they were in the west. I could not expect to enter upon the life of comfort which he would like so much to provide me. About the middle of January he came. When Cousin Nat came, he looked so handsome! And he wore a beautiful overcoat. I asked him secretly where he got it and learned that it was borrowed from his brother-in-law. I knew he was not able to buy a fine overcoat like that. He had sold two barrels of corn to get money with which to buy my wedding ring; moreover, he had borrowed a hundred dollars to use in case of emergency on such a long journey.

Mr. Crawford, pastor of the church in Arkadelphia of which Cousin Nat was a member and which I had attended, thought we would get him to perform the ceremony and told me he was going to make me promise to obey my husband. I told him I knew I never could obey anyone and I wasn't going to promise. So Mr. Carr, the Methodist minister, was engaged to marry us. He had already ridden twenty miles out of his way to tell me not to try to get Cousin Nat to change his opinion about his church and join the Methodist church with me, but that I should join the church with him, for he had observed that women could serve the Lord in any of our churches but a man, when he loses anchor, seldom makes a good church worker. I took his advice.

Our wedding day was set for January twenty-fourth; the twenty-fourth of January in '72 was beautiful. The weather had been balmy most of the winter until then. I remember there were white hyacinths blooming in the garden. I had no desire for the useless confusion attached to a big wedding. I was happy, though Honey was not there and though Pa walked off. Just before the ceremony I saw Pa slowly walking out toward the plum orchard. He would not see me married, dreading as he did to see me face a life of sacrifices and hardships. I never saw him again until I returned to Arkansas eleven years later.

Our bridal party was, however, a very merry one as Cousin Nat and I said goodbye to the dear ones at Sylvan Home and set out in a buggy to meet the stage at Tulip. Our luggage had been sent ahead on a wagon and Brother Tom went along on horse back to see that the wagon and buggy were returned home safe.

The stage did not leave Tulip until the next morning and we spent the night there with some friends. Before retiring I handed Cousin Nat the Bible and he had family prayers just as Pa had always done. And so, with the Book as our guide, we went on, facing a heavy snow storm, to travel by stage, rail, and private conveyance to my new home in North Carolina, where I have "lived happily ever after," and I am eighty.

Notes

1. Undated letter in the Harriet Bailey Bullock Daniel Collection, William R. Perkins Library, Duke University (hereafter referred to as Daniel Collection).

2. These letters are in the Daniel Collection.

3. Joan E. Cashin, *A Family Venture: Men and Women on the Southern Frontier* (New York and Oxford: Oxford University Press, 1991), 116–17.

4. The sources for this information are genealogical records of the Bullock family provided by Bailey Bullock Daniel's granddaughter, Dr. Bailey Webb of Durham, North Carolina, and a list of headstones in "The Bullock-McCaskill Cemetery" in *The Clark County Historical Journal* (hereafter referred to as *CCHJ*) (Winter 1979–80): 218.

5. See Jane Turner Censer, "Southwestern Migration Among North Carolina Planter Families: 'The Disposition to Migrate,'" *The Journal of Southern History*, Vol. LVII, No. 3 (August 1991): 417.

6. *Clark County Land Entries*,"Government Land Grants," Circuit Clerk's Office, Clark County Court House, Arkadelphia, Arkansas. Quoted in "The Settlement of Manchester," *CCHJ* (Winter, 1979–80): 19.

7. "The Settlement of Manchester," *CCHJ* (Winter 1979–80): 20.

8. Russell Pierce Baker, *Arkansas Township Atlas*, (Hot Springs: Arkansas Genealogical Society, 1984), 85.

9. Dallas County Tax Records, Microfilm Roll #45, Arkansas History Commission, Little Rock. Quoted in "Social and Economic Structure" (of Manchester), *CCHJ* (Winter 1979–80): 79.

10. Unpublished letter from S. V. Daniel to his sister Alice. Daniel Collection.

11. For discussion of the complex motives for migration, see Cashin, *A Family Venture*.

12. United States Bureau of the Census. Seventh Census, 1850, Schedule 4. Agriculture and Slave Schedules.

13. United States Bureau of the Census. Eighth Census, 1860. Arkansas. Agriculture and Slave Schedules.

14. Dallas County Deed Record, Book A, Microfilm Roll #31. Arkansas History Commission. Quoted in "Col. Charles Bullock, His Family and Home," *CCHJ* (Winter 1979–80): 209.

15. Sharon Luvois Shugart, "A Socioeconomic Analysis Of A Small Plantation in Dallas county, Arkansas, 1844–1868." (M. A. thesis, University of Arkansas, Fayetteville), 13.

16. Shugart, 59.

17. This description comes from a letter written to the editor by Neill McCaskill in June 1992.

18. Kimbrough Jones was born in North Carolina on 6 May 1803. He moved to Hardeman County, Tennessee, with his father Mathew and two brothers, Nathaniel Kimbrough Jones and Daniel Jones in 1827. He married Susan Trotter and they had three children. Kimbrough Jones died 12 April 1879; Susan Trotter Jones died 16 June 1896. They are buried in the Kimbrough Jones Cemetery, Clark County, Arkansas. Their house still stands. "The Kimbrough Jones Family And Home," *CCHJ* (Winter 1979–80): 192.

19. Jesse Read Harris was born 22 June 1810 in Montgomery County, Tennessee. On 26 April 1833, he married Rosannah McCauley. They had five children. Jesse Read Harris died 23 August 1892; Rosannah McCauley Harris died 16 December 1892. They are buried in Bethlehem Cemetery, Clark County, Arkansas. "The Jesse Reade Harris Family," *CCHJ* (Winter 1979–80): 232.

20. Alexander Wilson Littlejohn was born in Oxford, North Carolina, in 1811. He married Sarah Ann Walker and they moved

to Fayette County, Tennessee. They had nine children. Alexander Wilson Littlejohn died 16 June 1896; Sarah Ann Walker Littlejohn died 17 December 1900. They are buried in the Littlejohn Family Cemetery in Clark County, Arkansas. "The Littlejohn Family," *CCHJ* (Winter 1979–80): 223.

21. One wonders if Harriet may have gotten the time of this story confused. If Aunt Rose was truly a "stripling" when this happened, it is more likely that it took place when the family left North Carolina than when they left Tennessee. Moreover, Damon and Shadrack seem to be older in other accounts about them in this memoir than they could have been if they were this young when taken to Arkansas.

22. Thomas C. Hudson was born 20 September 1797 in Virginia, moved to Dickson county, Tennessee, as a child and then migrated to Fayette County, Tennessee, by 1826. He married Jamima (or Jemima) Tatum and they had ten children. On 25 August 1836 he purchased eighty acres of land in Clark County, Arkansas, and later bought an additional eighty acres. He was a practicing attorney, a major member of the Somerville Land Company and served in the Fourth and Fifth General Assemblies of Arkansas. Thomas C. Hudson died 9 October 1884; Jamima Tatum Hudson died 1 August 1886. They are buried in a small, lost for many years, graveyard in the woods in Clark County, Arkansas. "Thomas C. Hudson—Manchester Pioneer," *CCHJ* (Winter 1979–80): 140.

23. Nathan Strong was born 19 February 1789, in Henry County, Virginia, migrated to Lawrence County, Alabama, and there married Nancy Looney in 1821. They had six children who survived infancy. In 1836, Nathan Strong employed W. Radford McCargo to buy a section of land for him in Clark County, ten miles from the Ouachita River. The Strong family arrived in Clark County on 6 November 1837. Nathan Strong died 11 October 1863; Nancy Looney Strong died 30 June 1889. They are buried in the Strong Family Cemetery, Clark County, Arkansas. The house

Nathan Strong built still stands and is occupied by their descendants, the Claud McCaskill family. "The Nathan Strong Family," *CCHJ* (Winter, 1979–80): 154.

24. *L'eau Frais Creek* is the correct name of this stream. Stick chimneys were made of clay and laths or poles. "To build a stick and dirt chimney a framework of small poles was constructed in the shape of a chimney. These poles or sticks were one and a half or two inches in diameter and were placed horizontal in the framework much like the logs in a minature [*sic*] log cabin. Straw or grass was mixed with clay mud to hold the mud together. Starting at the bottom of the frame work, pieces of the mixture (cats they were called) the thickness of the cracks between the poles and about eight inches long were placed over the poles, half of the cat falling inside and half of it falling outside of the frame work. As soon as the frame work was covered with the cats, a big fire was built in the fireplace and the chimney 'cured' out. The fire hardened the clay in the cats and the fireplace was ready for use." Boyd W. Johnson (*The Arkansas Frontier*, n.p., 1957): 19.

25. Daniel E. Jones was born in North Carolina about 1810, married Ann Reagan and they had six children who survived to adulthood. He was the youngest brother of Kimbrough Jones and may have already been in the Manchester community when the Bullock party arrived in 1848. "A Few Jones Families" *CCHJ* (Winter 1979–80): 174. It is rather odd that Bailey remembers him as the *uncle* of Senator James K. Jones rather than as the *brother* of Kimbrough Jones, her father's good friend, who was also the Senator's uncle. Senator Jones was the son of Nathaniel K. Jones. All three brothers lived in the Manchester community when Bailey was a child.

26. See photographs and figures 3 and 4 for floor plans of the house.

27. This is one place where the manuscript and the typescripts do not agree. The typescripts say "I remember when Mr. Alex Littlejohn's house was the only painted one between the river and

Tulip." I have followed the manuscript because Harriet's description follows so closely another contemporary account of the Nathan Strong house which was finished about 1843. The Strong family tradition claims that as each of the sons reached the age of twenty-one he was sent to the fields to learn to "manage." "The house had two stories and six rooms. The first floor's four rooms were finished with plastered walls, the plaster carried from Malvern (Rockport) by oxcart. A 12 foot hall ran through the center of the house which had double doors at front and back. A small portico adorned the front and the house was painted white with green blinds, metal gutters, and lightning rods. All the woodwork, even the fine decorative moldings, was made by hand. The house was set on a twenty-acre lawn among oak trees." "The Nathan Strong Family," *CCHJ* (Winter, 1979–80): 154.

28. See figures 1 and 2 for site plans of the plantation houses and barns.

29. The two letters quoted in the Introduction, written to Harriet in 1917 by Eliza, one of the slaves listed in this poem, mention the whereabouts of some of the others.

30. Joseph Scott, according to the 1850 census, was then twenty-six years old and had been born in Alabama. After the Civil War he remained in the neighborhood and retained close ties with the Bullock family, although no longer employed as overseer. He is mentioned in family correspondence through the 1870s. Daniel Collection.

31. "This historic church (Bethlehem) is located seven miles east of Arkadelphia in the SE NE Sec. 21-7-18. The official date of its organization has been given as 1848 although, like many others, may have had its beginning several years earlier when members first met at their homes. Col. Charles Bullock was also an early member. After the death of his first wife in 1852, Colonel Bullock became a member of the Tulip Presbyterian Church where his name was entered on the roll in 1853. Shortly thereafter, with the help of a few others, he founded the Arkadelphia Presbyterian

Church where he remained as active member until his death. His second wife, Mary, was a member of the Bethlehem Church." "Bethlehem Methodist Church And Cemetery," *CCHJ* (Winter 1979–80): 43.

32. According to records of the First Presbyterian Church of Arkadelphia, the original members of the "Aid Society" that founded the church, were Col. Chas. Bullock, Mrs. Martha Rowland, Mrs. Martha Beattie, Mrs. Nancy Cossart, Mrs. Nancy Carmichael, Miss Flora Carmichael, Miss Mary Carmichael, Miss Martha Carmichael, and Mrs. Martha Flanagin. Col. Bullock and James Morehead were elders. Elizabeth McMillan, "Presbyterian Tales About the Life and Mission of First Presbyterian Church Arkadelphia, Arkansas," (pamphlet, May 9, 1989).

33. George Clark Eaton was born in Granville County, North Carolina, 3 March 1811. He married Elizabeth Harrison, born 1812, and they moved to Tulip Ridge about 1848. Jonathan K. Smith, *The Romance of Tulip Ridge* (Baltimore: Deford & Company,1966), 80.

34. Mary Jones would have been about seventeen at the time and Charles Bullock, about forty-one. She returned to Clark County and married first, R. L. Duff, who was only fourteen years her senior and then a Mr. Trotter. "The Kimbrough Jones Family And Home," *CCHJ* (Winter, 1979–80): 194.

35. "The Widow Gibson" was Nathan Strong's daughter, Maria Strong Gibson, who had married Thomas Jefferson Gibson of Rockport in 1844 and was widowed in 1850. At the death of Mr. Gibson, Maria and her only child, a daughter named Miller, and six slaves, returned to the Strong home to live. "The Nathan Strong Family," *CCHJ* (Winter, 1979–80): 157.

36. Mary Wilson Carter Bullock was born in North Carolina and is listed as age thirty-six in the 1860 census. She died in 1906 and is buried in the Charles L. Bullock Cemetery, Clark County, Arkansas. "The Bullock-McCaskill Cemetery" *CCHJ* (Winter, 1979–80): 218.

37. Calvin Jones, son of Kimbrough Jones, died 3 November 1857 at the age of twenty-four and is buried in the Kimbrough Jones Cemetery, Clark County, Arkansas. "The Kimbrough Jones Family And Home," *CCHJ* (Winter, 1979–80): 198.

38. These were the standard elementary school texts of the times. *McGuffey's Reader*, by William Holmes McGuffey, published by Truman and Smith is estimated to have sold 122,000,000 copies between 1836 and 1920. *The Elementary Speller*, known as "The Blue-Back Speller," published by Appleton, sold 35,000,000 copies between 1855 and 1890. Charles Davies' *First Lessons in Arithmetic* was first published in 1840 by A. S. Barnes and Company. Sir Isaac Watts' *Improvement of the Mind*, an eighteenth-century text much admired by Samuel Johnson, was printed in a number of places in America. Charles Carpenter Daniel, *History of American Schoolbooks.* (Philadelphia: University of Pennsylvania Press, 1963), 85, 140, 151, 240.

39. These fish, called "suckers," are easy to catch when they come into the shallows to spawn.

40. Jerusalem seeds were boiled and mixed with syrup to be given for worms. Turpentine and castor oil given together were given for malaria. Jack and Olivia Solomon, eds., *Cracklin' Bread and Asfidity: Folk Recipes and Remedies* (Tuscaloosa: University of Alabama Press, 1979), 142, 161. Sulphur and molasses were given together as a spring tonic. Ray B. Browne, *Popular Beliefs and Practices from Alabama* (Berkeley: University of California Press, 1958), 120.

41. One of the first churches organized in the Southwest, Manchester Methodist Church was organized by Rev. Jacob Custer in 1838. Charter members were Thomas C. and Jamima Hudson, Nathan and Nancy Strong, Miss Tennessee Hudson, Miss Moriah Strong, and one black member by the name of Laney. Church was held in their homes until a log church was built in 1844. "Early Churches and Preachers," *CCHJ* (Winter 1979–80): 40.

42. Reverend Andrew Hunter was born in 1813 in County

Antrim, Ireland, and died in Little Rock in 1902. He was one of the most colorful members of the Methodist pulpit for sixty-six years. In 1865 he was elected to the State Senate, where he served as President and while there was one of two senators elected to the United States Senate, a post he did not take because he did not feel he could abide by the oath required of Southerners at the time. Smith, *The Romance of Tulip Ridge*, 32.

43. It is impossible to identify this comet without knowing when it appeared, but it could not have been Halley's Comet which of course did not appear between 1835 and 1910. It may have been "The Great Comet" discovered in 1861 by Jerome L. Tebbett, described as being as bright as Saturn. This comet put on an impressive performance from 13 May until the end of August, 1861. On 30 June the earth apparently passed through the tail but despite some unconfirmed accounts of unusual daytime darkness and a yellowish sky, most reports indicated no perceptible effects. Gary W. Kronk, *Comets: A Descriptive Catalog* (Hillside, New Jersey: Enslow Publishers, Inc., 1984), 51.

44. The typescripts read "stood with him near the door." I have chosen the manuscript reading "around our beds" because this is what Bailey Daniel wrote and there is a significant difference between the two. The manuscript reading tells us something about the relationship between slave and master that we need to know.

45. According to the 1860 census, J. P. Tenney, physician, age forty-seven, was born in South Carolina. His wife, Mary A., age thirty-seven, was born in Georgia.

46. Otis Patton, a blind man, was made the first superintendent of the "Institute for the Education of the Blind" in 1859 and had to close the school for three years because of the war. He moved to Little Rock with the school in 1868 when it was renamed "The Arkansas School for the Blind." Bob Cowley Riley, "A Survey of the Education of the Young and Adult Blind in Arkansas with Recommendations for an Improved Program." (Ph.D. diss., University of Arkansas, Fayetteville, 1951). The church court

mentioned here probably took place while the institute was closed but before its removal to Little Rock. This would explain why the furnishings were still there.

47. Harris Flanagin (1817–1874) was the seventh governor of Arkansas, serving in the period 1862–64. Timothy Donovan and Willard B. Gatewood, Jr., eds., *The Governors of Arkansas* (Fayetteville: University of Arkansas Press, 1981), 33. It was his wife, Martha Elizabeth Nash Flanagin who helped Col. Bullock found the First Presbyterian Church in Arkadelphia.

48. A "twister" was apparently a stick the end of which could be twisted in the coat of an animal to pull it out of a hole or a tree.

49. Cards are small wooden pads with straight metal bristles about half-an-inch long. Before cotton could be spun, the fiber had to be "carded," or pulled between two cards as far as it would go.

50. According to the 1860 census, Peter Phillips, son of T. P. Phillips, was eighteen years old.

51. Judge Willis Lewis Somervell was born in Mecklenburg County, Virginia, 19 April 1811. He went to Hardeman County, Tennessee, as a young man and married Mary Ann Martin (1812–1893) in 1834. They moved to Tulip Ridge in 1834. During the Civil War they took refuge in Waco, Texas, with their slaves. Judge Somervell died there in 1864. Smith, *The Romance of Tulip Ridge*, 78.

52. Tom Bullock enlisted in Company I of the Third Arkansas Infantry, "The Tulip Rifles," a company of volunteers organized by Colonel George D. Alexander on 21 June 1861. According to the muster roll, Thomas Bullock enlisted as a private. Colonel Alexander had been the first superintendent of a military academy organized at Tulip in 1849, called "The Alexander Institute." However, by the beginning of the war he had become a planter. Smith, *The Romance of Tulip Ridge*, 52, 16.

53. Peyton Duke is listed in the 1860 census as a farmer, age fifty-one, born in North Carolina.

54. Figured at a minimum of four hundred pounds per bale this

cotton would have been worth $28,000, a considerable sum in 1865. However, they may well have been heavier bales, and so worth even more.

55. John Seldon Roane (1817–1867) served as the fourth governor of Arkansas in the years 1849–52. Donovan and Gatewood, *The Governors of Arkansas*, p. 33. The Rev. E. R. Barcus was head of the music department at the Methodist Seminary for young ladies in Tulip, and he and Mrs. Barcus supervised the boarding house for the girls. Smith, *The Romance of Tulip Ridge*, 24.

56. See figure 5. At Poison Spring on 18 April 1864, the Confederate cavalry, under Brigadier General Samuel B. Maxey, captured a Federal wagon train of some 225 wagons, 4 artillery pieces, and about 1500 men. Nearly 500 Federal troops, mostly black soldiers, were killed. "Report of Major General Sterling Price," John L. Ferguson, ed., *Arkansas and the Civil War* (Little Rock: Arkansas History Commission, 1962), 218.

57. See figure 5. The Bullock plantation was headquarters for Marmaduke's Cavalry Division during part of Steele's Camden Expedition, Brigadier General John Sappington Marmaduke (1833–1887) commanding. Brigade commanders were Brigadier General Joseph Orville Shelby (1830–1897) and Colonel Colton Greene. Two of General Shelby's dispatches, dated 3 May 1864, bear the return address "Camp Bullock," and "Camp at Bullock's." The Federal commander was Major General Frederick Steele (1819–1868). Ferguson, *Arkansas and the Civil War*, 223. Robert N. Scott, *The War of the Rebellion, Series I, Vol. xxxiv* (Washington, D.C.: Government Printing Office, 1901), 835–36.

58. R. L. Duff married Mary Jones, Kimbrough Jones' oldest daughter, the erstwhile object of Col. Bullock's affections. "The Kimbrough Jones Family And Home," *CCHJ* (Winter 1979–80): 194. He is listed in the 1870 census as a farmer, age fifty, born in Tennessee.

59. These were daughters of E. J. Phillips, listed in the 1860 census as a farmer, age forty-seven, born in North Carolina. Ellen was fifteen in the 1860 census.

60. Col. Colton Greene was a brigade commander under General Marmaduke. Ferguson, *Arkansas and the Civil War*, 223.

61. The soldier was obviously from a poor mountain farm where there would not have been slaves and where children had to work in the gardens and fields.

62. This plantation, Rosedale,was one of the largest in the area. Joseph Allen Whitaker (1812–1876) was born in North Carolina, married Rebecca Perry Yarborough and moved to Clark County in 1854. Smith, *The Romance of Tulip Ridge*, 82.

63. Dr. Lewis Downey Cooper, born in 1818 in Granville County, North Carolina, married Catherine Jane Yarborough (1825–1889) and they moved to Arkansas in 1845. Captain William Hunter Cooper served, with his two brothers, Joseph and James A. Cooper, in Company E of the second Arkansas. Smith, *The Romance of Tulip Ridge*, 55.

64. Julia A. Trigg, is listed in the 1860 census as age forty-two, born in Georgia, wife of James Trigg, farmer.

65. It should be noted that until Lee's surrender in April 1865, southern slaveowners tended not to consider "the matter settled" that the slaves would be freed. The Emancipation Proclamation, issued by President Lincoln to be effective 1 January 1863, could not be enforced outside the jurisdiction of the United States Army. The Bullock slaves apparently did not leave until after Lee's surrender.

66. Alsa J. Hunter was listed in the 1860 census as a merchant, age thirty-three, born in North Carolina.

67. In December 1856, the Tulip Female Collegiate Seminary, which had been chartered by the Arkansas Legislature on 17 December 1850, became a Methodist-sponsored school, serving the Ouachita Conference. The Rev. E. R. Barcus was head of the music department and with his wife supervised the boarding house for girls. Smith, *The Romance of Tulip Ridge*, 18, 24. This is also probably the school in which Miss Mary Cooper taught before the war.

68. This hapless couple must have been Robert W. (1830–1888)

and Elizabeth Mutter Littlejohn Hunter (1842–1915). She was the daughter of Alex Littlejohn. They seem to have been still living in this little house in 1872 when their son Alexander Littlejohn Hunter was born. The log house, subsequently covered with boards, was still standing in 1979. Their son Alexander must have prospered as he bought the Kimbrough Jones mansion on 590 acres on 16 August 1909. "The Kimbrough Jones Home After Its Purchase By The Hunter Family," *CCHJ* (Winter 1979–80): 200.

69. This store, known as "H. Palmer and Co. Drug Store," was located on the northeast corner of Main and Fifth streets in Arkadelphia in 1865. Duncan Flanagin, "Map and Guidebook of Arkadelphia, 1865," *CCHJ* (Fall 1987): 65.

70. Mary Connerly (1835–1908) was a "Yankee Schoolmarm" who got bottled up in Camden by the war. In 1865 she went to Arkadelphia to teach in a school run by Samuel Stephenson, bought the school in 1869 and named it "The Arkadelphia Female College," which she operated until 1874, when she returned to her home, Newburg, New York. She was so highly thought of that long after she had left Arkadelphia some of her former pupils started a literary club named in her honor. Farrar Newberry, "The Yankee Schoolmarm Who 'Captured' Post-war Arkadelphia," *Arkansas Historical Quarterly*, XVII, No. 4 (Winter, 1958): 267.

71. Nathaniel Beverly (1842–1909) and Venable Daniel were the sons of Ann Harriet Bullock (Charles Bullock's sister) and Nathaniel Chesley Daniel.

72. The usual route had been by carriage to Pine Bluff where a steamer was boarded for a trip down the Arkansas River to Napoleon, a port town at the juncture of the Arkansas and Mississippi Rivers where a different steamer was boarded for the journey up the Mississippi to Memphis. By this time, however, Napoleon was crumbling into the Mississippi, so she may have made the change at Arkansas City.

73. According to information in family letters to Bailey by her sisters who remained in Arkansas, Dr. Palmer apparently bought

some of this land from Mr. Bullock who retained a portion for himself. The return address on letters mailed from the Palmer place was Belle Flower, Arkansas. Daniel Collection.

74. Edward Cross was a State Supreme Court Justice and a U.S. Congressman. *Biographical and Historical Memoirs of Southern Arkansas* (Chicago, Nashville, and St. Louis: The Goodspeed Publishing Co., 1890), 382. Judge Cross is listed in the 1860 census as a farmer and his son, Homer C., is listed as being nineteen years of age. Mary Helen and Homer went to live in Hempstead County.

Bibliography

Baker, Russell Pierce. *Arkansas Township Atlas*. Hot Springs:
     Arkansas Genealogical Society, 1984.
"Bethlehem Methodist Church And Cemetery," *Clark County
     Historical Journal* (hereafter referred to as *CCHJ*) (Winter
     1979–80): 272–74.
Biographical and Historical Memoirs of Southern Arkansas. Chicago,
     Nashville, and St. Louis: The Goodspeed Publishing Co.,
     1890.
Browne, Ray B. *Popular Beliefs and Practices from Alabama*. Berkeley:
     University of California Press, 1958.
"The Bullock-McCaskill Cemetery," *CCHJ* (Winter 1979–80):
     217–22.
Cashin, Joan E. *A Family Venture: Men and Women on the Southern
     Frontier*. New York and Oxford: Oxford University Press,
     1991.
Censer, Jane Turner. "Southwestern Migration Among North
     Carolina Planter Families: 'The Disposition to Migrate,'" *The
     Journal of Southern History* LVII No. 4 (August 1991): 407–26.
Clinton, Catherine. *The Plantation Mistress*. New York: Pantheon,
     1982.
"Col. Charles L. Bullock, His Family and Home," *CCHJ* (Winter
     1979–80): 205–17.
Daniel, Charles Carpenter. *History of American Schoolbooks*.
     Philadelphia: University of Pennsylvania Press, 1963.
Daniel, Harriet Bailey Bullock. Unpublished Letters in the Harriet
     Bailey Bullock Daniel Collection. William R. Perkins
     Library, Duke University.
Donovan, Timothy, and Willard B. Gatewood, Jr. *The Governors of
     Arkansas*. Fayetteville: University of Arkansas Press, 1981.

"Early Churches and Preachers," *CCHJ* (Winter 1979–80): 39–60.

Ferguson, John L., ed. *Arkansas and the Civil War*. Little Rock: Arkansas History Commission, 1962.

"A Few Jones Families," *CCHJ* (Winter 1979–80): 173–79.

Fox-Genovese, Elizabeth. *Within the Plantation Household*. Chapel Hill and London: University of North Carolina Press, 1988.

"The Jesse Reade Harris Family," *CCHJ* (Winter 1979–80): 232.

Johnson, Boyd W. *The Arkansas Frontier*. N.p. 1957.

"The Kimbrough Jones Family And Home," *CCHJ* (Winter 1979–80): 192–97.

"The Kimbrough Jones Home After Its Purchase By The Hunter Family," *CCHJ* (Winter 1979–80): 200–204.

Kronk, Gary W. *Comets: A Descriptive Catalog*. Hillside, New Jersey: Enslow Publishers, Inc., 1984.

"The Littlejohn Family," *CCHJ* (Winter 1979–80): 223–28.

McMillan, Elizabeth, "Presbyterian Tales About the Life and Mission of First Presbyterian Church Arkadelphia, Arkansas." 9 May 1989 (pamphlet).

"Map and Guidebook of Arkadelphia, 1865," *CCHJ* (Fall 1987): 53–76.

"The Nathan Strong Family," *CCHJ* (Winter 1979–80): 154–63.

Newberry, Farrar. "The Yankee Schoolmarm Who 'Captured' Post-War Arkadelphia," *Arkansas Historical Quarterly* XVII (Winter 1958): 267.

Riley, Bob Cowley. "A Survey of the Education of the Young and Adult Blind in Arkansas with Recommendations for an Improved Program." Ph.D. diss., University of Arkansas, Fayetteville, 1951.

Scott, Robert N. *The War of the Rebellion*. I, xxxiv. Washington, D.C.: Government Printing Office, 1901.

"The Settlement of Manchester," *CCHJ* (Winter 1979–80): 16–22.

Shugart, Sharon Luvois. "A Socioeconomic Analysis of a Small Plantation in Dallas County, Arkansas, 1844–1868." M.A. thesis, University of Arkansas, Fayetteville, 1990.

Smith, Jonathan K. *The Romance of Tulip Ridge*. Baltimore: Deford & Company, 1966.

"Social and Economic Structure" (of Manchester), *CCHJ* (Winter 1979–80): 77–85.

Solomon, Jack and Olivia, eds. *Cracklin' Bread and Asfidity: Folk Recipes and Remedies*. Tuscaloosa: University of Alabama Press, 1979.

"Thomas C. Hudson—Manchester Pioneer," *CCHJ* (Winter 1979–80): 140–45A.

United States Bureau of the Census. Seventh Census, 1850. Agriculture, Population, Slave Schedules.

United States Bureau of the Census. Eighth Census, 1860. Agriculture, Population, Slave Schedules.

United States Bureau of the Census. Ninth Census, 1870. Population Schedule.

Index of Names

Bell, 65, 89
Betsy, 35, 49, 66, 68, 78, 85
Betsy Ann, 36
Bill, 35
Billy, 34, 35, 41, 50, 64, 65–66, 77
Cat, 36, 40
Ceily, 36
Charles Lewis, 35
Clary, Aunt, 4
Clay, 35
Damon, 29–30, 35, 44, 74,
  75–76, 137 n. 21
Dan (Tuck), 35
Delia, 36
Dick, 35, 36
Edmund, 35
Eliza, 4–6, 34, 35, 44, 139 n. 29
Emily, 34, 36, 65
Eva, 36
Fanny, 35
Fed, 34, 35, 36
Grace, 35, 97
Goodlow, Betsy Ann, 6
Hannah, 36
Harriet, 6, 36
Harry, 6, 35
Henry, 5, 35
Ida, 89
Jenny, 34, 35, 64
Jerry, 5, 35, 36, 98
Joe, 36
John (Aunt 'Riah's husband left
  in North Carolina), 33
John W., 34
Jones, Jim, 6
June, 35, 75–76
Kemp, 35
Leah, 34, 36
Letty, 36, 49
Line (Caroline), 6, 36
Lizzy, 35, 44
Lucy, 29–30, 36

Macklin, 35, 89
Martha, 35
Martha Ann, 6
Matilda, 35
Nancy, 6
Nelly, 36
Oscar, 6, 35, 102
Patsy, 4, 49, 71, 97, 102
Phil, 35
Pollyanna, 35
Priscilla, 35
Rachel, Aunt, 4, 6, 8, 34, 35,
  72–73
Rebecca, 35
'Riah (Moriah), 8, 33–34, 35, 39,
  40, 41, 44, 47, 66–67, 68, 70–71,
  74, 84, 92, 93, 101, 112, 129
Robert, 35
Rose, Aunt, 4, 6, 8, 29–30, 34,
  35, 44, 58, 59, 61–62, 63, 65,
  77–78, 137 n. 21
Sam, 6, 35, 36
Shadrack, 29–30, 35, 74, 137 n. 21
Silla, 6
Polly, 6, 34
Tiny, 36, 102
Vick, 6, 36
Victoria, 36

Carmichael, Flora, 140 n. 32
Carmichael, Martha, 140 n. 32
Carmichael, Mary, 140 n. 32
Carmichael, Nancy, 140 n. 32
Carter, Mary Wilson, 12
Carr, Reverend, 133
Cashin, Joan, 8, 136 n. 11
Cleveland, Lafayette, 79
Cleveland, Zeb, 79
Clinton, Catherine, 9
Colburn, Sammy, 109, 110
Connerly, Mary, 115–16, 118, 119,
  146 n. 70

Hunter, Alsa J., 102, 145 n. 66
Hunter, Reverend Andrew, 62,
    63–64, 74, 141–42 n. 42
Hunter, Elizabeth Mutter Littlejohn
    (Mrs. Robert W.), 145–46 n. 68
Hunter, Robert W., 104, 145–46 n.
    68

Ivy, Mr., 92

Jefferson, Johnny, 127
Jefferson, Mr., 126
Johnson, Samuel, 141 n. 38
Jones, Anna, 29
Jones, Calvin, 29, 56, 141 n. 37
Jones, Daniel, 31–32, 136 n. 18, 138
    n. 25
Jones, Elihu, 79
Jones, Senator James K., 31, 138 n.
    25
Jones, Kim, 79
Jones, Kimbrough, 12, 13, 14, 29,
    31, 33, 44–45, 47, 62, 75, 81, 94,
    136 n. 18, 141 n. 37, 145–46 n.
    68
Jones, Mary, 29, 44–45, 79, 140 n.
    34, 144 n. 58
Jones, Nathaniel K., 14

Lambeth, Laura, 13
Lee, Robert E., 83, 102, 145 n. 65
Levy, Helen, 61
Lincoln, Abraham, 145 n. 65
Littlejohn, Alexander Wilson, 12,
    13, 29, 37, 81, 136–37 n. 20,
    138–39 n. 27
Littlejohn, Betty, 103–04
Littlejohn, Willie, 79
Littlejohn, Zan, 79

MacBride, D. D., 108
MacCallum, I. B., 108

McCaskill, Alex, 12
McCaskill, Becky, 109, 110
McCaskill, Clara, vii, 23
McCaskill, Claude, vii, 23
McCaskill, Neill, vii, 10, 13, 19, 23,
    136 n. 17
McCaskill, Wilson Ella, 109, 110
McGuffey, William Holmes, 141 n.
    38
Marmaduke, General John
    Sappington, 93, 144 n. 57, 145 n.
    60
Maxey, General Samuel B., 144 n.
    56
Mills, Billy, 84–85
Mitchell, Margaret, 1
Morehead, James, 43, 140 n. 32

Palmer, Arianna Booker Bullock
    (Sister Anna Booker); *see*
    Bullock, Arianna Booker
Palmer, Horace Dr., 12, 88–90, 96,
    113, 125, 146 n. 69
Palmer, Sarah, 103
Patton, Otis, 129, 142–43 n. 46
Phillips, E. J., 144 n. 59
Phillips, Ellen, 94, 144 n. 59
Phillips, Peter (Pony), 79, 143 n. 50
Pratt, Mr., 102
Price, General Sterling, 144 n. 56
Pryor, Dan, 40

Richter, Wendy L., viii
Reid, Mary Taylor, 124, 126–27
Roane, Governor John Seldon, 87,
    144 n. 55
Rowland, Martha, 140 n. 32

Scott, Joseph Hinton, 36, 46, 50,
    62, 66, 69, 74, 75, 86, 99, 112,
    139 n. 30
Shapherd, Robert, 29

Shapherd (Shaphard, Shaperd),
Thomas, 28, 29, 47
Shapherd, Mrs. Thomas
(Grandma), 72, 120
Shelby, General Joseph Orville, 93,
94, 98, 99, 144 n. 57
Shugart, H. F., 23
Shugart, Sharon Luvois, 23
Singleton, Johnny, 116
Slaves, *see* Bullocks, slaves belong-
ing to
Sommervel, Judge Willis Lewis, 82,
143 n. 51
Sordo, Olivia, viii
Steel, Dr., 79, 80
Steele, General Frederick, 99, 144
n. 57
Strong, Lany, 64
Strong, Nancy Looney, 137–38 n.
23, 141 n. 41
Strong, Nathan, 10, 31, 45, 62,
137–38 n. 23, 138–39 n. 27, 141
n. 41
Stowe, Harriet Beecher, 96

Taylor, Edmund, 124
Taylor, Samuel L., 12, 83, 124

Taylor, John Robert, 108
Taylor, Sara Catherine Bullock
(Sister Kate); *see* Bullock, Sara
Catherine
Tenney, Dr. J. P., 66, 67, 142 n. 45
Tenney, (Mrs. J. P.), 67, 142 n. 45
Throckmorton, Governor Jim, 16
Tinny, Virgie, 79
Trigg, James, 37, 145 n. 64
Trigg, Julia A., 37, 99, 145 n. 64
Trotter, Mr., 140 n. 34

Ward, Pleasant, 18
Webb, Arianna Shapherd, 28
Watts, Sir Isaac, 141 n. 38
Webb, Bailey, vii, 20–21, 22, 135 n.
4
Whitaker, Joseph Allen, 99, 145 n.
62
Whitaker, Rebecca Perry
Yarborough (Mrs. Joseph Allen
Whitaker), 145 n. 62
Wilks brothers, 92
Williams, W. L., 13
Witherspoon, Mrs., 43
Wright, Jo, viii